When Growth Becomes A Burden

Freeing Pastors from False Measures of Church Success

Bishop Dr. Antonio M. Palmer, D.Div

WHEN GROWTH BECOMES A BURDEN

Freeing Pastors from False Measures of Church Success

Published by:

Kingdom Publishing LLC

1350 Blair Drive, Suite F, Odenton, MD 21113

Printed in the United States of America

Copyright ©2026 by Antonio M. Palmer

ISBN: 978-1-967006-24-3 (Paperback)
ISBN: 978-1-967006-25-0 (Ebook)

Unless otherwise indicated, all Scripture quotations in this book are taken from the King James Version (KJV) of the Bible.

The King James Version is in the public domain in the United States; therefore, no special permissions are required for its use. All biblical references have been cited in their original wording to preserve the theological, historical, and literary tone most familiar within traditional pastoral and ecclesial contexts.

Any occasional paraphrases or summaries of biblical passages are the author's own and are intended solely for explanatory purposes.

TABLE OF CONTENTS

Dedication

This book is dedicated to all pastors who have accepted their call to the sacred ministry of the church and have chosen to live out their calling in faithfulness and sincerity.

Acknowledgements

No work like this is written alone. It is shaped by voices, relationships, and faithful leaders who labor quietly for the sake of others.

I extend my sincere gratitude to Archbishop Ralph Dennis and Bishop Courtney McBath for their steadfast leadership, spiritual mentorship, and unwavering support of pastors around the world—especially those who serve in difficult, unseen, and often overwhelming contexts. Your commitment to strengthening weary leaders and restoring hope to the called has left an indelible mark on the global body of Christ.

I am also deeply thankful to Bishop Frank L. Holloman for his faithful partnership and assistance in encouraging and strengthening the pastors of the Kingdom Alliance of Churches International. Your wisdom, presence, and willingness to walk alongside leaders have been a tremendous blessing.

To each of you, thank you for modeling leadership that is grounded not in visibility, but in faithfulness—and for reminding pastors everywhere that they are not alone.

With gratitude and honor,

Antonio M. Palmer

Foreword

I have walked beside ministry long enough to know that what most people see is rarely the whole story.

They see the sermons, the services, the celebrations. They see the moments when growth is visible and milestones are reached. What they do not always see are the long nights, the quiet frustrations, the prayers whispered when no one is watching, and the weight a pastor carries when faithfulness feels heavier than fruitfulness.

I have seen those things—up close.

I have lived them as a pastor's wife.

For more than three decades, I have watched my husband give himself to the work God entrusted to him. I have watched him preach with passion to full rooms and to half-empty ones. I have watched him labor faithfully in seasons when growth came steadily and in seasons when it seemed to stall. I have watched him wrestle—honestly and prayerfully—with the same questions many pastors ask in private: *Am I doing enough? Am I missing something? Does this still matter?*

This book was not written from theory. It was written from life.

I have seen the burden ministry can place on a pastor's heart—not because he lacks faith, but because he loves God and God's people deeply. I have seen how easily expectations—spoken and unspoken—can weigh on a leader. I have watched how comparison, if left unchecked, can quietly steal joy from obedience.

But I have also seen faithfulness.

I have seen what it looks like to keep going when applause is minimal and progress feels slow. I have seen the quiet victories that never make announcements—the restored marriages, the healed hearts, the leaders raised, the prayers answered in time rather than immediately.

Most importantly, I have witnessed a journey of transformation.

I have seen my husband grow from pastor, to shepherd, to spiritual father. I have watched his leadership mature—not driven by ambition, but shaped by obedience. I have seen him learn when to push forward and when to wait; when to speak boldly and when to listen patiently; when to lead from the front and when to walk beside others.

That kind of growth does not happen overnight. It is formed through faithfulness across seasons.

As a pastor's wife, I know how ministry growth affects more than just the leader—it affects the family. I have felt the tension of expansion and the strain of responsibility. I have known the relief when growth was handled wisely and the exhaustion when it was not. I have learned that growth without grace can wound a household, while faithfulness grounded in God's timing can strengthen it.

This book speaks to those realities with honesty and compassion.

It does not shame pastors for wanting to see fruit. It does not diminish the value of growth. Instead, it gently but firmly reframes the conversation—calling pastors back to what truly sustains them: obedience, trust, and intimacy with God.

I believe this book is necessary.

I believe it will heal places pastors rarely talk about. It will give language to burdens many carry silently. It will remind leaders that their worth is not measured by numbers, platforms, or comparisons—but by faithfulness to Christ.

To the pastor reading this: you are seen. Your labor matters. Your obedience is not wasted. And you are not alone.

My prayer is that as you turn these pages, you will feel permission—to rest where you need to rest, to release what you were never meant to carry, and to rediscover the joy of serving God without fear.

This book is not just a message—it is an invitation. An invitation to breathe again. To lead lighter. To trust deeper.

And to believe, with renewed confidence, that **well done** truly is greater than **well known**.

— Dr. Barbara A. Palmer
Kingdom Celebration Center
Gambrills, MD

Preface

I did not intend to write a book about growth.

I intended to write a book about pastors.

Over the years, I have listened to countless conversations—some spoken openly, others whispered quietly—where faithful shepherds wrestled with a single, haunting question: Why does ministry feel heavier than it should? For many, the answer was not a loss of faith, discipline, or calling. It was the growing weight of expectations placed upon them—expectations often measured by numbers rather than obedience.

At some point, growth stopped feeling like a blessing and started feeling like a burden.

I have pastored for more than three decades. I have walked with congregations through joy and sorrow, increase and decrease, clarity and confusion. I have led a local church that never crossed the thresholds often celebrated in ministry culture, yet remained deeply committed to loving God, serving people, and proclaiming truth. And now, as a bishop, I have the privilege of fathering and encouraging pastors across dozens of churches—many of them small, faithful, and largely unseen.

What I have learned is this: the burden many pastors carry is not the absence of growth, but the presence of false measures of success.

Pastors are rarely discouraged because they are unfaithful. More often, they are discouraged because they are faithful in systems that reward visibility more than obedience. They labor week after week, preach the Word, shepherd people, pray, counsel, bury the dead, dedicate the young, and stand faithfully at their post—yet quietly wonder if their work still "counts" because their numbers do not match someone else's.

This book was born out of those conversations.

It is written for pastors who love Jesus deeply but feel the constant weight of comparison. For shepherds who are faithful in small places. For leaders who have resisted the temptation to perform but still feel the pressure to produce. For those who sense that something about modern success metrics feels misaligned with Scripture, yet struggle to articulate why.

Let me be clear: this book is not an argument against growth. Growth matters. Scripture affirms increase, fruitfulness, and multiplication. But growth becomes dangerous when it is detached from faithfulness—and burdensome when it becomes the primary measure of worth.

Jesus never asked His servants to be impressive.

He asked them to be faithful.

When Christ evaluated His churches, He did not ask how many they gathered, how influential they appeared, or how visible they were. He examined their love, their obedience, their endurance, their repentance, and their faithfulness. That alone should give every pastor pause—and relief.

My prayer is that this book will free pastors from carrying burdens they were never meant to bear. That it will replace pressure with perspective, shame with clarity, and exhaustion with renewed confidence in Christ's calling. That it will remind every reader that success in ministry is not determined by scale, but by stewardship.

If growth has become a burden to you, this book is an invitation to lay that burden down—and to take up the lighter, truer yoke of faithfulness.

May we all be found faithful.

Bishop Antonio M. Palmer
Kingdom Alliance of Churches International
Presiding Prelate

Introduction

"Come unto me, all ye that labour and are heavy laden,
and I will give you rest."
— Matthew 11:28 (KJV)

Growth was never meant to be a burden.

In the beginning, growth was a blessing. It was spoken by God, promised by covenant, and celebrated as evidence of life. From the first pages of Scripture, increase is associated with God's creative intent—fruitfulness flowing naturally from alignment with His purposes. Yet somewhere along the way, particularly within modern ministry culture, growth quietly changed categories. What was once received as fruit became demanded as proof. What was once celebrated as grace became expected as performance. And for many pastors, growth—especially numerical growth—has become not a joy, but a weight.

This book is written for those pastors.

It is written for shepherds who did not enter ministry to compete, compare, or perform, yet find themselves evaluated— sometimes subtly, sometimes overtly—by numbers they do not fully control. It is written for leaders who love Christ deeply, labor faithfully, and still feel the unspoken pressure to justify their calling through attendance figures, budgets, buildings, or visibility. It is written for pastors who carry a burden they were never meant to bear.

The Quiet Weight Pastors Carry

Most pastors will never publicly admit that growth has become a burden. Ministry culture rewards confidence, optimism, and vision. To confess discouragement can feel like spiritual failure or leadership weakness. And yet, beneath the surface of many faithful ministries lies a quiet exhaustion—not from the work of shepherding itself, but from the constant sense of being measured by standards that feel disconnected from Scripture.

The burden often shows up subtly. It appears in the comparison that creeps in after scrolling through ministry updates online. It surfaces in denominational reports that equate health with expansion. It emerges in well-meaning questions—How many members do you have now? Are you growing?—that unintentionally communicates that numbers tell the whole story.

Sociological research confirms what many pastors already know intuitively: the majority of churches in the United States are small. Studies from the National Congregations Study and the Pew Research Center consistently show that most Protestant congregations have fewer than 100 regular attendees, with a large share under 75.[1] This reality, however, rarely shapes the dominant narrative of success in ministry. Instead, the most visible models—often megachurches with extensive resources—become the unspoken benchmark against which all churches are measured.

The result is predictable. Faithful pastors begin to question their effectiveness. Long-term obedience feels overshadowed by short-term outcomes. Shepherding gives way to strategizing. Prayer becomes pressured. And growth—once a sign of God's blessing—becomes a burden pastors feel responsible to produce.

When Metrics Replace Meaning

The problem is not measurement itself. Scripture is not opposed to evaluation, accountability, or stewardship. The apostle Paul regularly assessed the fruit of his labor, and the early church counted converts as the gospel spread (Acts 2:41; 4:4). The problem arises when what we measure begins to redefine why we minister.

Modern ministry culture often borrows its metrics from organizational and corporate frameworks, where success is defined by scale, efficiency, and expansion. These tools are not inherently evil, but they are insufficient—and often harmful— when applied uncritically to the life of the Church. When numerical growth becomes the primary indicator of success, it subtly reshapes pastoral identity. Pastors move from being stewards of souls to managers of outcomes. Faithfulness becomes secondary to visibility. And obedience is quietly replaced by optimization.

Scripture offers a very different framework.

In 1 Corinthians 3, Paul confronts a church obsessed with personalities and outcomes. He reminds them that while leaders plant and water, *"God giveth the increase"* (1 Corinthians 3:6 KJV). Growth, in Paul's theology, is ultimately God's work. Human responsibility lies in faithfulness, not results. Later in the same letter, Paul crystallizes this principle: *"Moreover it is required in stewards, that a man be found faithful"* (1 Corinthians 4:2 KJV). Faithfulness—not growth—is the requirement.

Gordon Fee notes that Paul's emphasis on stewardship intentionally shifts attention away from external success and toward accountability before God.[2] Ministers are answerable not to public opinion or comparative metrics, but to the Lord who entrusted them with their assignment.

Jesus and the Refusal to Perform

If modern ministry culture elevates growth as proof of success, the ministry of Jesus presents a striking contrast. Jesus drew crowds—sometimes in the thousands—yet He never oriented His mission around retaining them. In fact, at several pivotal moments, He spoke in ways that intentionally sifted His audience. John's Gospel records that after one particularly challenging teaching, "many of his disciples went back, and walked no more with him" (John 6:66 KJV).

From a modern perspective, this moment might be labeled a leadership failure. Jesus did not clarify His message to maintain engagement. He did not soften His language to preserve momentum. He did not appear concerned with the optics of decline. Instead, He turned to the twelve and asked a deeply pastoral question: Will ye also go away? (John 6:67).

Jesus was not managing a crowd; He was forming disciples.

This distinction matters. Crowds respond to attraction. Disciples respond to obedience. When growth becomes the primary goal, discipleship often becomes collateral damage. Dietrich Bonhoeffer warned of this danger in *The Cost of Discipleship*, arguing that when grace is preached without demand, the result is "cheap grace"—belief without obedience, belonging without transformation.[3] Churches can grow numerically while shrinking spiritually.

The Churches Jesus Evaluated

Perhaps the clearest biblical corrective to false measures of church success is found in Revelation 2–3. In these chapters, the risen Christ addresses seven churches in Asia Minor. These churches varied widely in context, strength, and challenge. Some were persecuted. Others were compromised. Some were faithful but weary. Yet one detail is unmistakable: Jesus never mentions attendance, budgets, or influence.

Instead, Christ evaluates each church based on spiritual criteria—love, faithfulness, repentance, endurance, doctrinal integrity, and obedience. To Ephesus, He commends labor but confronts lovelessness. To Smyrna, He offers encouragement amid suffering. To Laodicea, He rebukes complacency and self-sufficiency. In every case, the evaluation is moral and covenantal, not numerical.

Craig Koester observes that Revelation presents Jesus as the One who "walks among the churches," intimately aware of their condition and unwavering in His standards.[4] His concern is not how churches appear, but who they have become. If numerical growth were the primary measure of success, Revelation would have been the place for Jesus to say so. He does not.

Faithfulness and the Long Obedience

Throughout Scripture, God's servants are repeatedly commended not for visible success, but for steadfast obedience. Noah preached righteousness for decades before a single drop of rain fell. Jeremiah proclaimed God's word faithfully while facing rejection, imprisonment, and isolation. The author of Hebrews recounts men and women who lived by faith yet "received not the promise" in their lifetime (Hebrews 11:39).

Eugene Peterson famously described Christian discipleship as "a long obedience in the same direction."[5] This phrase captures the essence of pastoral faithfulness. Ministry is not a sprint fueled by novelty, but a pilgrimage shaped by perseverance. Yet perseverance rarely looks impressive. It often unfolds quietly—in hospital rooms, counseling sessions, prayer meetings, funerals, and small gatherings of faithful believers.

When growth becomes a burden, it is often because pastors have been taught—explicitly or implicitly—to value visibility over longevity. The biblical narrative, however, consistently honors those who endure.

The Hidden Strength of Small Churches

Small churches are frequently described in terms of deficiency—what they lack in resources, staff, or reach. Rarely are they celebrated for their unique strengths. In smaller congregations, pastors often know their people by name and story. Shepherding is personal, not programmatic. Accountability is relational. Discipleship happens through proximity.

Nancy Ammerman's research on congregational life highlights that smaller churches often exhibit deeper relational bonds and stronger community integration than their larger counterparts.[6] These congregations may not generate headlines, but they often sustain faith across generations.

The early church itself was not a centralized megastructure, but a network of local assemblies—often meeting in homes—connected through apostolic oversight and shared doctrine. Growth occurred organically, through witness, hospitality, and perseverance under pressure. Alan Kreider argues that the early church's expansion was driven less by strategy and more by patient faithfulness lived out in daily life.[7]

Reframing Growth and Releasing the Burden

The central claim of this book is simple but demanding: growth becomes a burden when it is detached from faithfulness. When pastors feel responsible to produce outcomes that belong to God alone, ministry becomes heavy. When success is defined by borrowed metrics, obedience feels insufficient. But when faithfulness is restored as the primary measure, the burden begins to lift.

This does not mean abandoning vision, evangelism, or discipleship. It means reordering them. Growth is not rejected; it is reclaimed as fruit rather than function. Some churches will grow numerically. Others will grow in depth, stability, or generational impact. Still others may remain small yet faithful for decades, serving as anchors of witness in their communities. Each expression has value when it flows from obedience rather than comparison.

The Purpose of This Book

This book is written to free pastors from false measures of church success. It seeks to restore biblical perspective, pastoral confidence, and spiritual rest. The chapters that follow will explore how Scripture defines growth, what Jesus expects from His Church, how the early church functioned, and how pastors can pursue health without surrendering to pressure.

Above all, this book is an invitation—to lay down burdens Christ never assigned, and to take up the lighter yoke of faithfulness He promises (Matthew 11:30).

If growth has become a burden, it is not because you are failing. It may be because you are measuring yourself by standards Jesus never gave.

And that burden can be laid down.

When Size Was Never the Measure

For the first three centuries of Christianity, the Church had **no buildings, no state support, and no public legitimacy.** Growth occurred through households, relationships, and witness—often under threat of persecution. Success was measured by **faithfulness under pressure**, not numerical dominance. Only after Constantine (4th century) did institutional size and visibility begin to influence perceptions of legitimacy.

Reflection Prayer

Faithful God,

You see the weight I carry—some of it given by You, some of it I have assumed. Forgive me for measuring my obedience by outcomes rather than trust. Quiet the voices that demand more than You require. Teach me again what it means to serve You freely, without fear, without comparison. Let this journey begin not with striving, but with surrender.

Amen.

Chapter 1
When Growth Becomes a Burden

"For my yoke is easy, and my burden is light."
— Matthew 11:30 (KJV)

There is a moment in many pastors' lives when the joy of ministry begins to feel heavy. Not because they no longer love God, and not because they no longer care for people, but because something subtle has shifted in how success is defined. The work is still holy. The calling is still clear. Yet the weight feels different. What once felt like privilege now carries pressure. Growth— once prayed for with hope—begins to feel like an expectation that must be met, explained, or defended.

This is the moment when growth becomes a burden.

It rarely announces itself loudly. It does not arrive with a resignation letter or a public confession. Instead, it creeps in quietly—through comparison, through metrics, through questions that sound innocent but linger heavily. How many people attend your church? Are you growing? What's your five-year plan? These questions, repeated often enough, can reshape how pastors see themselves and how they evaluate their faithfulness.

The tragedy is not that pastors desire growth. That desire is biblical. The tragedy is that many pastors begin to shoulder responsibility for outcomes that Scripture reserves for God alone.

The Burden Jesus Never Assigned

Jesus was clear about the nature of the burden He gives. "Come unto me," He said, "all ye that labour and are heavy laden, and I will give you rest" (Matthew 11:28 KJV). He did not promise the absence of work, but He did promise a different kind of weight. His yoke, He insisted, is easy—not because discipleship is effortless, but because it is rightly shared. The burden of obedience belongs to the disciple; the burden of outcome belongs to God.

Yet in modern ministry culture, these burdens are often reversed. Pastors labor faithfully, but rest feels elusive. Anxiety replaces assurance. Prayer becomes pressured. Sermon preparation is subtly influenced by what might "work" rather than what is true. And beneath it all lies a nagging sense that faithfulness alone may no longer be enough.

This tension reveals a theological misunderstanding. Scripture never assigns pastors the responsibility to produce growth. It assigns them the responsibility to steward what has been entrusted to them. Paul articulated this distinction clearly when addressing the Corinthian church: "I have planted, Apollos watered; but God gave the increase" (1 Corinthians 3:6 KJV). The verbs matter. Human leaders plant and water; God alone gives increase. When pastors attempt to carry what belongs to God, the result is inevitable—burden.

Gordon Fee observes that Paul's argument in this passage is intentionally corrective, aimed at dismantling a success-driven view of ministry that elevates leaders based on visible results rather than faithful service.[1] The church in Corinth was enamored with outcomes and personalities, and Paul redirected their attention to God's sovereign role in growth. The same redirection is needed today.

How Comparison Fuels the Burden

One of the most powerful accelerants of pastoral burden is comparison. In previous generations, pastors compared themselves primarily within their immediate denominational or geographic context. Today, comparison is global and constant. Social media, livestreams, conferences, and curated success stories place pastors in a perpetual state of measurement—often against ministries with vastly different contexts, resources, and callings.

The apostle Paul warned explicitly against this tendency: "For we dare not make ourselves of the number, or compare ourselves with some that commend themselves: but they measuring themselves by themselves, and comparing themselves among themselves, are not wise" (2 Corinthians 10:12 KJV). Comparison distorts wisdom because it shifts the reference point from obedience to optics.

When pastors compare outcomes rather than assignments, faithfulness begins to feel insufficient. A church that is healthy, loving, and stable can feel like a failure simply because it is not expanding numerically. This distortion does not arise from Scripture; it arises from culture.

Sociological studies confirm that most churches are small, yet visibility is disproportionately given to large congregations. Mark Chaves notes that American religious life is shaped more by typical congregations than by exceptional ones, yet narratives of success are overwhelmingly drawn from the margins rather than the middle.[2] The result is a skewed imagination of what "normal" ministry looks like—and an unnecessary burden placed on pastors who are faithfully serving typical congregations.

When Metrics Replace Shepherding

The shift from shepherding to measuring is subtle but consequential. Shepherding is relational, slow, and often unseen. Measuring is numerical, fast, and easily communicated. When growth metrics dominate ministry conversations, pastors may begin to prioritize what can be counted over what must be cultivated.

Scripture consistently portrays pastoral leadership using the language of shepherding. Jesus identified Himself as the Good Shepherd who knows His sheep and lays down His life for them (John 10:11–14). Peter exhorted church leaders to "feed the flock of God… not as being lords over God's heritage, but being ensamples to the flock" (1 Peter 5:2–3 KJV). Shepherding is about care, presence, and protection—not performance.

Yet when growth becomes a burden, pastors may feel pressured to exchange shepherding for strategizing. Time once devoted to prayer and people is consumed by planning and promotion. Faithfulness is redefined as productivity. And ministry begins to resemble management more than pastoral care.

This shift does not produce healthier churches. It produces tired pastors.

Jesus and the Courage to Lose Crowds

Few moments in the Gospels confront growth-driven assumptions more sharply than John 6. After feeding the five thousand, Jesus experienced a surge of popularity. Crowds followed Him eagerly, yet He refused to allow their enthusiasm to redefine His mission. When He taught about the cost of discipleship, many turned away. Rather than adjusting His message, Jesus allowed the departure—and then turned to the twelve.

From a contemporary perspective, this moment feels counterintuitive. Leadership literature often emphasizes momentum, retention, and scaling. Jesus emphasized truth, obedience, and transformation. He did not measure success by how many stayed, but by whether those who stayed were willing to follow.

Dietrich Bonhoeffer's warning about "cheap grace" speaks directly to this dynamic. Grace that demands nothing produces discipleship that costs nothing—and churches that grow without depth.[3] Jesus refused to build a movement sustained by misunderstanding or convenience. His ministry reminds pastors that faithfulness may sometimes result in decrease before it results in fruit.

The Churches Jesus Confronted and Commended

Revelation 2–3 offers perhaps the clearest evidence that growth is not Christ's primary concern. In His messages to the seven churches, Jesus evaluates faithfulness, doctrine, love, endurance, and repentance. He praises perseverance, rebukes compromise, and calls for renewal. He never references attendance or influence.

Craig Koester emphasizes that these letters reveal Christ's intimate knowledge of each congregation's condition.[4] He addresses them not as institutions to be scaled, but as communities to be shepherded. Some churches are small and suffering. Others are comfortable and complacent. All are accountable.

This should be profoundly liberating for pastors. If Jesus does not measure His churches by size, why should His servants?

The Myth of Uniform Growth

One of the most damaging assumptions in modern ministry is the belief that all faithful churches should grow in the same way and at the same pace. Scripture offers no such promise. The New Testament presents diversity, not uniformity. Churches met in homes, cities, and regions. Some grew rapidly; others endured quietly. Apostolic oversight provided unity of doctrine, not uniformity of expression.

Alan Kreider's research on the early church shows that growth often occurred slowly, organically, and without a centralized strategy.[5] The early Christians did not possess marketing tools or institutional power. They bore witness through embodied faithfulness—often at great cost. Growth followed witness, not the other way around.

When pastors expect uniform outcomes, they unintentionally deny the contextual nature of God's work. What faithfulness produces in one place may differ greatly from what it produces in another. Growth becomes a burden when pastors feel compelled to force outcomes rather than discern assignments.

Faithfulness as Freedom

The freedom this book seeks to recover is not freedom from responsibility, but freedom from false responsibility. Pastors are responsible to preach the Word, love the people, steward their gifts, and obey Christ. They are not responsible to manufacture results.

Eugene Peterson's description of ministry as "a long obedience in the same direction" captures this freedom well.[6] Faithfulness unfolds over time. It resists the urgency of immediate results and trusts God with the harvest. This perspective does not diminish vision; it purifies it.

When faithfulness becomes the metric, pastors are released from the tyranny of comparison. They are free to serve the church they have been given rather than chasing the church they imagine they should have. Growth, when it comes, is received as grace—not carried as burden.

Naming the Burden So It Can Be Laid Down

This chapter names the burden because burdens cannot be laid down until they are acknowledged. Many pastors have carried unnecessary weight for years, believing it to be part of the calling. It is not. Jesus never asked His servants to prove their worth through numbers. He asked them to follow Him.

When growth becomes a burden, it is often a sign that success has been misdefined. This book exists to help pastors recover a biblical definition—one rooted in faithfulness, obedience, and trust.

The chapters that follow will continue this work. We will examine how growth became synonymous with success, how Scripture reframes that assumption, and how pastors can lead healthy churches without surrendering to pressure or performance.

For now, hear this clearly: if growth feels heavy, it may not be because you are failing. It may be because you are carrying something Christ never placed on your shoulders.

And that burden can be laid down.

Constantine and the Shift in Church Expectations

After Christianity became legal in the Roman Empire (313 AD), churches began receiving buildings, funding, and political favor. With this shift came a subtle change: visibility began to replace faithfulness as a marker of success. Bishops gained influence, congregations grew rapidly, and numerical size slowly became associated with divine approval—an assumption foreign to the persecuted early church.

Reflection Prayer

Lord Jesus,

You invited the weary to come to You—not to perform for You. Reveal the burdens I have carried that are not Yours. Teach me to lay down expectations rooted in fear or pride. Restore joy to my obedience and lightness to my calling. I choose Your yoke, not mine.

Amen.

Chapter 2

Is Megaministry God's Will for Everyone?

"There are diversities of operations, but it is the same God which worketh all in all."

— 1 Corinthians 12:6 (KJV)

Few questions create as much confusion—and quiet insecurity—among pastors as this one: If God is blessing my ministry, shouldn't it be bigger by now? Beneath that question lies another, rarely voiced but deeply felt: Is megaministry the goal I somehow missed?

In a ministry culture saturated with stories of rapid expansion, national platforms, and global reach, it is easy to assume that size is not merely one possible outcome of faithfulness, but the expected outcome. The implication is subtle yet powerful: if a church remains small or modest, something must be wrong—with the pastor, the vision, or the level of faith. Over time, this assumption hardens into a theology of inevitability: If God is truly at work, growth must look a certain way.

This chapter challenges that assumption—not to diminish growth, but to restore discernment.

Calling Is Not a Carbon Copy

Scripture presents calling as deeply personal and contextually specific. God does not issue identical assignments to all His servants. Moses was called to lead a nation. Jeremiah was called to speak to a nation—often without visible response. Ezekiel was warned in advance that his audience would resist him, yet obedience was still required (Ezekiel 2:5–7). The measure of faithfulness was never uniform outcomes, but unwavering obedience.

The apostle Paul's ministry alone defies simplistic growth formulas. In some cities, churches flourished quickly; in others, Paul faced intense opposition and limited fruit. At times he preached to large crowds; at other times he labored quietly, supporting himself through tentmaking (Acts 18:1–4). Paul never interpreted varied outcomes as evidence of inconsistent calling. He understood that assignment, not applause, defined his work.

This biblical pattern reveals an uncomfortable truth: faithfulness does not guarantee scale. God distributes assignments according to His wisdom, not according to human expectations. When pastors assume that megaministry is the normative goal, they inadvertently flatten the diverse callings Scripture celebrates.

The Rise of a Singular Ministry Ideal

The idea that successful churches must be large is not primarily biblical; it is cultural. In the modern Western context, size often functions as a proxy for legitimacy. Large organizations are assumed to be effective. Small ones are presumed to be struggling. These assumptions, drawn from corporate and consumer frameworks, have quietly shaped ecclesial imagination.

Sociological research highlights this distortion. While the vast majority of churches are small, the stories that dominate conferences, books, and media platforms are drawn from a small percentage of exceptionally large congregations.[1] These stories are often inspiring, but when presented without context, they create unrealistic expectations. The exceptional becomes the expected. The result is a ministry culture that celebrates scalability while marginalizing sustainability.

Scripture never endorses a single ministry ideal. Instead, it affirms diversity of gifts, operations, and outcomes—"the same God which worketh all in all" (1 Corinthians 12:6 KJV). Uniformity of size is neither promised nor required.

Jesus and the Myth of Universal Expansion

If megaministry were God's universal will, Jesus Himself would be its clearest model. Yet the Gospels resist that conclusion. Jesus' ministry drew crowds, but He consistently refused to organize His mission around expansion. He did not build an institution designed to scale rapidly. He invested deeply in a small group of disciples, often withdrawing from crowds rather than cultivating them.

When asked to perform signs to satisfy popular demand, Jesus declined. When crowds attempted to make Him king, He withdrew (John 6:15). His kingdom was not built through spectacle, but through obedience, sacrifice, and truth. Jesus demonstrated that impact and size are not synonymous.

This does not mean Jesus opposed growth. It means He refused to let growth define success. His focus remained fixed on faithfulness to the Father's will, even when that faithfulness limited public appeal.

The Seven Churches and the Absence of Size

The messages of Revelation 2–3 offer a sobering corrective to size-driven ministry expectations. Jesus addresses seven churches—each with a unique context and condition. Some are strong but loveless. Others are weak yet faithful. Some are compromised by comfort; others are refined by suffering. In every case, Jesus evaluates character, doctrine, endurance, and obedience. He never evaluates size.

This omission is striking. If numerical growth were the universal expectation for churches, Revelation would be the moment for Christ to clarify that standard. Instead, He speaks as a shepherd examining the heart of each congregation. Faithfulness, not footprint, is His concern.

This should recalibrate pastoral imagination. Churches are accountable to Christ for who they are becoming, not for how large they appear.

Assignment Determines Outcome

One of the most liberating truths for pastors is the recognition that assignment determines outcome. God assigns different fields, different seasons, and different measures of fruit. Jesus illustrated this reality in the parable of the sower, where the same seed produces varying yields depending on the soil (Matthew 13:8). The seed is consistent; the results are not.

When pastors confuse assignment with ambition, they place themselves under unnecessary strain. They attempt to force growth patterns that do not align with their context. They adopt strategies designed for environments vastly different from their own. And when the results do not match expectations, discouragement follows.

The apostle Paul resisted this temptation. He understood his apostolic assignment as pioneering work—laying foundations where Christ was not yet known (Romans 15:20). Others were called to build upon those foundations. Both roles were necessary; neither was superior.

In the same way, some pastors are called to plant and pioneer. Others are called to stabilize and shepherd. Some are called to multiply through sending. Others are called to sustain through presence. Each assignment carries dignity when it is received from God rather than borrowed from culture.

The Cost of Chasing the Wrong Calling

When pastors pursue a vision not given to them, the cost is often hidden but severe. Burnout increases. Families feel the strain. Churches become restless. Ministry becomes performative rather than pastoral. The burden grows heavier because the work no longer aligns with grace.

Research on pastoral burnout consistently identifies unrealistic expectations and role overload as significant contributors.[2] When pastors feel compelled to meet externally imposed standards— often tied to growth metrics—they experience increased stress and decreased satisfaction. The calling becomes a grind rather than a gift.

This is not a failure of faith; it is a misalignment of calling.

Small, Faithful, and Fully Obedient

Scripture offers numerous examples of ministries that remained small yet faithful. The prophetic ministries of Jeremiah and Ezekiel were not marked by widespread repentance, yet they were unquestionably obedient. John the Baptist's ministry prepared the way for Christ but diminished once Jesus' ministry emerged (John 3:30). John did not resist obscurity; he embraced it as obedience.

These examples challenge the assumption that growth is always upward and outward. Sometimes faithfulness requires remaining where one is planted, tending the same soil year after year. Sometimes it involves decrease, not expansion. Jesus Himself taught that losing one's life is the pathway to finding it (Matthew 16:25). This paradox applies not only to individuals, but to ministries.

Megachurches Without Mythology

This chapter is not an indictment of large churches. Many megachurches are faithful, well-led, and deeply committed to the gospel. They steward significant resources and reach vast numbers of people. Their existence is not the problem. The problem arises when their outcomes are treated as the universal standard.

When megaministry becomes mythology—an idealized destination for every pastor—it distorts calling. It implies that God's favor is measured in square footage and seating capacity. It subtly communicates that smaller churches are merely waiting rooms for "real" success.

Scripture does not support this hierarchy. The body of Christ requires diversity, not duplication. The health of the whole depends on the faithfulness of each part (1 Corinthians 12:14–26).

Freedom Through Discernment

The question is not whether God can grow a church. He can. The question is whether growth—defined in a particular way—

is what God has assigned you to steward. Discernment replaces comparison. Obedience replaces anxiety. Faithfulness replaces fear.

When pastors embrace their assignment, growth no longer feels burdensome. They labor diligently without striving. They plan wisely without performing. They trust God with outcomes because they know they are walking in obedience.

This is freedom—not freedom from responsibility, but freedom from false expectations.

Reclaiming the Right Question

The most important question for pastors is not How big should my church be? but What has Christ asked me to steward faithfully? When that question guides ministry, the burden lifts. Success is no longer borrowed from another context. It is defined by obedience.

This chapter invites pastors to release the myth of universal megaministry and to recover a biblical understanding of calling and assignment. Growth may come. It may not. But faithfulness remains the measure.

The next chapter will turn our attention to how Jesus Himself evaluates churches—examining the criteria He uses and the priorities He reveals. In doing so, we will continue the work of freeing pastors from false measures of success and anchoring ministry in Christ's own assessment.

Monastic Movements: Faithful but Small

From the 3rd–10th centuries, monastic communities flourished across Africa, the Middle East, and Europe. These communities rarely grew large, yet they **preserved Scripture, theology, prayer, and discipleship** through centuries of instability. Their faithfulness shaped Christianity more profoundly than many large urban churches of their time.

Reflection Prayer

God of all assignments,

Deliver me from the temptation to envy another calling. Help me steward faithfully what You have entrusted to me. Give me clarity about my assignment and contentment in my obedience. May I honor Your work in every size, every place, every season.

Amen.

Chapter 3
What Jesus Actually Measures

"I know thy works."
— Revelation 2:2 (KJV)

If pastors were to strip ministry down to its most essential question, it would not be How many came? or How much did we grow? The question that matters most—because it is the one Christ Himself asks—is far simpler and far more searching: What do I see when I look at you?

The book of Revelation opens with a sobering reality often overlooked in contemporary ministry culture: Jesus walks among His churches. He does not evaluate them from a distance, nor does He rely on reports, statistics, or secondhand accounts. He sees. He knows. And He speaks with authority born of intimacy. Each of the seven messages in Revelation 2–3 begins with the same arresting phrase: "I know thy works." Not I know your attendance, or I know your influence, but I know your works.

This chapter is about reclaiming Christ's evaluation of His Church—and allowing His criteria to reshape how pastors measure faithfulness and success.

The Weight of Being Seen by Christ

There is comfort and conviction in Jesus' words. Comfort, because nothing done in faithfulness is hidden from Him. Conviction, because nothing is concealed either. Christ's evaluation is thorough, personal, and exact. He addresses each church individually, acknowledging their strengths and confronting their failures. He does not offer a generic assessment. He speaks to this church, in this place, with this history.

This reality should reorient pastoral imagination. Ministry is not primarily performed before people; it is lived before Christ. The audience that ultimately matters is singular. The pressure to impress dissipates when pastors remember who is watching.

Craig Koester notes that the repeated declaration "I know" emphasizes Christ's intimate knowledge of each congregation's lived reality.[1] Jesus evaluates not reputation, but reality. This distinction matters profoundly in an age where perception can easily overshadow substance.

The Seven Churches as Christ's Scorecard

The seven churches—Ephesus, Smyrna, Pergamum, Thyatira, Sardis, Philadelphia, and Laodicea—represent a spectrum of spiritual conditions. They were real congregations, facing real challenges, within a specific historical context. Yet their inclusion in Scripture signals that their evaluation carries enduring significance for the Church in every generation.

What is striking is not merely what Jesus says, but what He does not say. Across all seven letters, there is no mention of numerical size, financial strength, or cultural influence. Christ's concerns are moral, relational, and covenantal.

Let us briefly consider the categories Jesus consistently measures.

Love and Devotion

To the church in Ephesus, Jesus offers a paradoxical assessment. He commends their labor, perseverance, and doctrinal vigilance. They have tested false apostles and endured hardship. Yet in the midst of commendation comes a piercing rebuke: "Nevertheless I have somewhat against thee, because thou hast left thy first love" (Revelation 2:4 KJV).

Ephesus appears successful by many standards. They are active, discerning, and resilient. But something essential is missing. Love—devotion to Christ—has cooled. Jesus' warning is severe: without repentance, their lampstand will be removed.

This moment exposes a dangerous possibility: a church can be busy, orthodox, and resilient, yet deficient in love. Activity does not compensate for affection. Growth does not substitute for devotion. Jesus measures the heart before the hands.

The pastoral implication is clear. Churches can grow in complexity while shrinking in intimacy. Faithfulness requires guarding love, not merely sustaining programs.

Faithfulness Under Pressure

The church in Smyrna receives no rebuke—only encouragement. They are poor, afflicted, and slandered, yet Jesus declares them rich (Revelation 2:9). Their faithfulness is measured not by expansion, but by endurance. They are suffering, not scaling. Yet Christ's assessment is unequivocal: they are faithful.

This letter dismantles the assumption that blessing always looks like growth. Smyrna's poverty and persecution are not signs of divine displeasure; they are the context in which faithfulness shines most clearly. Jesus does not promise relief from suffering, but He promises reward for endurance.

For pastors serving in difficult contexts—declining communities, hostile environments, or seasons of scarcity—Smyrna stands as a powerful reminder that Christ's approval is not contingent on favorable conditions. Faithfulness under pressure is fully seen and fully honored.

Truth and Compromise

Several churches are evaluated based on their relationship to truth. Pergamum is commended for holding fast to Christ's name, even in a place described as "where Satan's seat is" (Revelation 2:13). Yet they are rebuked for tolerating false teaching. Thyatira is praised for love and service, but confronted for permitting moral compromise.

These letters reveal that Jesus measures not only what churches affirm, but what they tolerate. Truth is not merely confessed; it is guarded. Love is not merely expressed; it is disciplined. Churches that grow numerically while compromising doctrinal or moral integrity may appear successful externally, but they fail Christ's evaluation internally.

Dietrich Bonhoeffer warned that when the Church abandons costly obedience, it exchanges discipleship for accommodation.[2] The letters to Pergamum and Thyatira confirm this warning. Jesus calls His churches to repentance not because He delights in judgment, but because faithfulness demands alignment.

Spiritual Vitality Versus Reputation

The church in Sardis receives perhaps the most sobering assessment of all: "Thou hast a name that thou livest, and art dead" (Revelation 3:1 KJV). Reputation and reality are at odds. From the outside, Sardis appears alive. From Christ's vantage point, it is spiritually lifeless.

This distinction should arrest every pastor. Churches can cultivate an image of vitality while lacking true spiritual life.

Programs can run smoothly. Attendance can be respectable. Yet beneath the surface, prayer can be absent, repentance neglected, and dependence on the Spirit replaced by routine.

Jesus' call to Sardis is not to grow, but to wake up. Revival begins not with expansion, but with awakening. Growth that precedes vitality is hollow. Christ measures life, not image.

Endurance and Opportunity

Philadelphia is another church that receives unqualified praise. They possess little strength, yet they keep Christ's word and do not deny His name (Revelation 3:8). Jesus places before them an open door—an opportunity for witness—not because they are large, but because they are faithful.

This moment reframes opportunity itself. Doors open not merely because churches are resourced, but because they are reliable. Faithfulness creates trust. Trust invites responsibility. Responsibility precedes increase.

For pastors laboring faithfully with limited resources, Philadelphia offers hope. Christ's assignment is not constrained by human weakness. He entrusts opportunity to those who will steward it well.

Self-Sufficiency and Spiritual Blindness

Laodicea represents the danger of comfort and self-reliance. They are wealthy, secure, and confident. Yet Jesus describes them as wretched, miserable, poor, blind, and naked (Revelation 3:17). Their problem is not size or scarcity, but self-sufficiency. They believe they have need of nothing.

This church illustrates how success—by worldly standards— can dull spiritual awareness. Comfort breeds complacency.

Prosperity can mask poverty of soul. Jesus' counsel is not to grow, but to repent and return to dependence.

The pastoral lesson is sobering: growth can become a liability if it produces self-reliance rather than humility. Christ measures dependence as much as diligence.

Works as Evidence, Not Currency

Across all seven letters, Jesus repeatedly affirms works. He is not indifferent to action. Yet works function as evidence of faithfulness, not as currency for approval. Christ does not weigh churches on a scale of productivity; He examines the nature and motivation of their labor.

This aligns with the broader New Testament witness. James insists that faith expresses itself through works (James 2:17). Paul affirms that believers are created for good works prepared by God (Ephesians 2:10). Yet neither apostle equates works with merit. Obedience flows from relationship, not from performance.

When growth becomes a burden, it is often because works are treated as currency—something pastors must accumulate to justify their calling. Jesus dismantles this framework. He measures works as fruit of faithfulness, not as proof of worth.

Christ's Authority to Evaluate

One reason Christ's evaluation carries such weight is His authority. In Revelation, Jesus is depicted as the risen Lord—holding the keys of death and hell, walking among the lampstands, speaking with the authority of the Son of God. His judgments are not arbitrary; they are covenantal. He addresses His churches as One who purchased them with His blood.

This covenantal context matters. Jesus evaluates not as a distant inspector, but as a faithful Bridegroom and Shepherd. His rebukes aim at restoration. His warnings invite repentance. His promises call for perseverance.

The purpose of Christ's evaluation is not condemnation, but correction.

Releasing False Metrics

When pastors allow Christ's criteria to shape their understanding of success, false metrics lose their power. Attendance, budgets, and buildings may still matter—but they are no longer ultimate. They become tools to steward, not standards to chase.

The freedom this chapter invites is profound. Pastors are free to ask different questions: Are we loving Christ deeply? Are we guarding truth faithfully? Are we shepherding people well? Are we enduring with integrity? Are we dependent on the Spirit?

These are the questions Jesus asks.

Living Under Christ's Gaze

To live and lead under Christ's gaze is both humbling and liberating. It humbles because it removes the illusion of control. It liberates because it clarifies responsibility. Pastors are accountable for faithfulness, not for outcomes.

This chapter calls pastors back to that clarity. Christ still walks among His churches. He still speaks. He still knows.

And what He measures is far more meaningful—and far more merciful—than the metrics that often burden His servants.

The next chapter will turn our attention to a necessary clarification: how small churches can be both faithful and healthy without being stagnant, and why size alone tells an incomplete story of spiritual vitality.

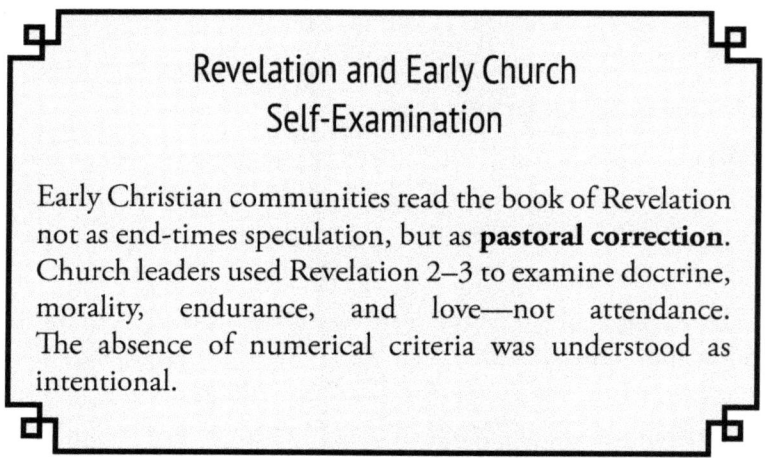

Revelation and Early Church Self-Examination

Early Christian communities read the book of Revelation not as end-times speculation, but as **pastoral correction**. Church leaders used Revelation 2–3 to examine doctrine, morality, endurance, and love—not attendance. The absence of numerical criteria was understood as intentional.

Reflection Prayer

Rigtheou Judge,

Search my heart as You searched the churches of old. Where love has cooled, restore it. Where endurance is strained, strengthen it. Where obedience has wavered, realign me. Teach me to value what You value and to trust Your evaluation above all others.

Amen.

Chapter 4
Small Does Not Mean Stagnant

"Despise not the day of small things."
— Zechariah 4:10 (KJV)

Few assumptions have done more quiet damage to the confidence of pastors than the belief that small automatically means stuck. In many ministry conversations, size is treated as a spiritual diagnostic. Growth is assumed to signal health; lack of numerical expansion is presumed to indicate deficiency. Over time, this assumption hardens into an unspoken verdict: if a church remains small, it must be failing—or at best, waiting for something better.

Scripture offers no support for this conclusion.

This chapter confronts the myth that small churches are inherently stagnant and argues instead that smallness and faithfulness are not opposites. A church may be small and healthy, modest and obedient, limited in size yet rich in spiritual vitality. When numerical growth is treated as the sole indicator of progress, pastors are burdened with expectations God never gave, and congregations are robbed of confidence in their present assignment.

The Cultural Bias Against Smallness

Western culture is deeply shaped by scale. Bigger is assumed to be better. Faster is equated with success. Visibility is mistaken for value. These assumptions did not originate in Scripture; they emerged from economic and industrial frameworks that prize expansion, efficiency, and market share. When imported into the Church without discernment, they distort theology and pastoral identity.

Sociologist Mark Chaves notes that while the typical American congregation is small, public imagination is dominated by a handful of large, highly visible churches.[1] This distortion creates a false norm. What is statistically ordinary becomes spiritually suspect. Faithful pastors leading ordinary congregations begin to feel extraordinary pressure to justify their calling.

Yet Scripture repeatedly affirms that God often works most powerfully through what appears small, weak, or unimpressive.

God's Pattern of Small Beginnings

The biblical narrative consistently resists the glorification of scale. God chooses the younger son over the elder, the shepherd boy over the seasoned warrior, the remnant over the multitude. Gideon's army is deliberately reduced so that victory cannot be attributed to human strength (Judges 7:2). David's kingship begins in obscurity. Jesus Himself is born in a manger, raised in Nazareth, and gathers a small group of disciples rather than a mass movement

Zechariah's exhortation—"Despise not the day of small things"—was spoken to a post-exilic community discouraged by modest beginnings. The people longed for visible glory, yet God called them to faithfulness in rebuilding what appeared insignificant (Zechariah 4:6–10). The message was clear: divine purpose is not determined by initial scale.

Walter Brueggemann observes that biblical faith regularly calls communities to trust God's work in unremarkable spaces, resisting the temptation to equate significance with spectacle.[2] This pattern directly challenges modern assumptions about church size and vitality.

Small Churches in the New Testament World

The New Testament church was not born large. It was born fragile. Early Christian communities met primarily in homes, not public halls. These gatherings were intimate, relational, and often vulnerable. Growth occurred, but it unfolded through witness, hospitality, and perseverance rather than centralized programming.

Wayne Meeks' seminal work on early Christian social life demonstrates that house churches functioned as extended families, marked by shared meals, mutual care, and strong relational bonds.[3] These communities were small by necessity, yet they proved resilient under persecution and remarkably effective in sustaining faith across generations.

Alan Kreider further argues that the early church's growth was largely unintentional. Christians did not pursue expansion as a strategy; they pursued faithful living. Growth followed witness, not planning.[4] This challenges modern models that treat numerical increase as the primary objective rather than a secondary fruit.

Health Versus Expansion

One of the most damaging assumptions in ministry is the conflation of growth with health. While healthy organisms tend to grow, growth alone does not guarantee health. Cancer grows rapidly; maturity develops slowly. Scripture consistently prioritizes health—right relationship with God and one another—over expansion.

The pastoral epistles emphasize character, doctrine, and stability far more than numerical outcomes. Paul instructs Timothy and Titus to appoint leaders of proven faithfulness, sound doctrine, and moral integrity (1 Timothy 3; Titus 1). These qualifications are deeply relational and ethical. None are numerical.

Gordon Fee notes that Paul's vision for church life is rooted in formation rather than accumulation.[5] Churches are to be shaped into mature communities reflecting Christ, not evaluated by external markers alone.

Small churches often excel in precisely these areas. Proximity allows for accountability. Shepherding is personal. Discipline is relational rather than bureaucratic. These strengths are not signs of stagnation; they are indicators of health.

The Hidden Strengths of Small Churches

Small churches possess assets that are often overlooked or undervalued:

- Relational depth: Members are known, not numbered.
- Pastoral presence: Shepherds are accessible and involved.
- Community integration: Churches are embedded in local life rather than operating as destinations.
- Stability: Long-term relationships foster resilience and trust.

Nancy Ammerman's research highlights that smaller congregations often demonstrate stronger internal cohesion and higher levels of member participation than larger churches.[6] These qualities contribute to long-term sustainability, even when numerical growth is modest.

Ironically, when small churches attempt to imitate large-church models, they often undermine their own strengths. Programs designed for scale can overwhelm limited resources. Metrics intended for large systems can obscure meaningful progress. The result is frustration rather than faithfulness.

When Smallness Is Mistaken for Failure

The danger arises when pastors internalize the belief that smallness equals inadequacy. This belief fuels discouragement and distorts calling. Faithful shepherds begin to view their ministry as a placeholder rather than a purpose. The present assignment is endured rather than embraced.

Scripture offers a corrective. In the parable of the talents, Jesus commends servants not for producing equal outcomes, but for faithful stewardship according to what they were given (Matthew 25:14–30). The servant entrusted with two talents receives the same commendation as the one entrusted with five. Faithfulness—not scale—is the measure.

This principle dismantles hierarchical thinking about church size. A small church faithfully stewarded is not inferior to a large church faithfully stewarded. Each is accountable to Christ according to its assignment.

The Danger of Forced Growth

When pastors believe their churches must grow numerically to be legitimate, they may attempt to force growth through strategies misaligned with their context. Programs are added without capacity. Vision is borrowed without discernment. Expectations rise without infrastructure. Growth, when it comes, becomes unsustainable; when it does not, discouragement deepens.

Research on pastoral burnout consistently identifies misaligned expectations as a significant contributor to emotional exhaustion.[7] When pastors pursue outcomes disconnected from their calling or context, ministry becomes heavy. Small churches are particularly vulnerable to this dynamic, as they often lack the systems necessary to absorb rapid expansion.

Healthy growth must be contextual. What is appropriate for a congregation of two thousand may be destructive for a congregation of fifty. Wisdom lies not in imitation, but in discernment.

Fruit That Cannot Be Counted

Some of the most significant fruits of ministry are not immediately visible or measurable. Faith formed over decades. Marriages strengthened quietly. Children raised in the faith. Leaders developed and sent. Communities served consistently. These outcomes rarely appear in annual reports, yet they reflect deep faithfulness.

James reminds the Church that patience is essential to maturity (James 1:4). Formation takes time. Growth that bypasses formation produces instability rather than strength. Small churches, precisely because they move at a slower pace, are often well-positioned for this kind of enduring fruit.

Reclaiming Confidence in the Present Assignment

This chapter calls pastors to reclaim confidence in the church they are presently called to serve. Smallness is not a deficit to overcome; it is a context to steward. Faithfulness in small places matters deeply to God. Scripture affirms this truth repeatedly.

When pastors release the false equation of size with success, they are free to labor with joy rather than anxiety. They are free to shepherd rather than perform. Growth—whether numerical or otherwise—returns to its proper place as fruit, not burden.

The next chapter will explore how the early church model challenges modern assumptions about growth and structure, further reinforcing the biblical vision of faithfulness over scale.

The Donatist and Desert Churches of North Africa

In North Africa (3rd–5th centuries), many faithful Christian communities remained small yet spiritually rigorous. These churches emphasized holiness, discipline, and perseverance under persecution. Their influence extended beyond their size, shaping African Christian theology and practice for generations.

Reflection Prayer

God of the mustard seed,

Forgive me for despising small beginnings or quiet seasons. Help me see Your work clearly—even when it is hidden. Teach me to honor faithfulness where You have planted me. Let me shepherd without apology and serve without shame.

Amen.

Chapter 5
The Early Church Was Not a Franchise

"And daily in the temple, and in every house, they ceased not to teach and preach Jesus Christ."

— Acts 5:42 (KJV)

One of the most persistent myths shaping modern church growth conversations is the belief that the early church expanded through a centralized, uniform, and highly organized system that can be easily replicated today. This myth fuels the assumption that growth is primarily the result of adopting the right model, implementing the right systems, or following the right leadership blueprint. Churches that do not scale in predictable ways are often viewed as deficient rather than different.

The New Testament tells a different story.

The early church did not grow through franchising. It grew through faithfulness. It did not spread because it perfected strategy, but because it embodied conviction. It was not standardized, but deeply contextual. And most importantly, it was not driven by performance metrics, but by devotion to Christ, obedience to the Spirit, and perseverance under pressure.

This chapter dismantles the assumption that the book of Acts provides a replicable growth formula and instead recovers its true purpose: to testify to what God did through a Spirit-formed community living faithfully in the midst of opposition.

Acts Is Testimony, Not Template

The book of Acts is often approached as a manual for church growth. Attendance figures are highlighted. Miracles are cataloged. Expansion is celebrated. While Acts certainly records moments of dramatic numerical increase, it does not present those moments as a repeatable strategy. Luke writes as a historian and theologian, not as a consultant. His aim is to bear witness to the work of the risen Christ through the Holy Spirit, not to prescribe a universal organizational model.

Richard Bauckham reminds readers that Acts must be read as theological narrative—a testimony to God's mission unfolding through real people in real places.[1] Luke describes what happened; he does not instruct readers to reproduce every detail. When modern churches treat Acts as a blueprint rather than a witness, they risk misapplying descriptive moments as prescriptive mandates.

This distinction matters. What God did in Jerusalem at Pentecost occurred within a unique historical, cultural, and covenantal moment. The influx of thousands was connected to pilgrimage festivals, shared language, and a concentrated population already familiar with Israel's Scriptures. To assume that such growth should be normative in every context is to ignore the specificity of God's work.

House Churches and Relational Networks

The dominant structure of the early church was not the public auditorium, but the household. Believers gathered in homes to pray, break bread, receive teaching, and care for one another

(Acts 2:46; Romans 16:5; Colossians 4:15). These gatherings were intimate, relational, and deeply embedded in everyday life.

Wayne Meeks' research into early Christian communities demonstrates that house churches functioned as extended families, shaped by shared meals, mutual responsibility, and strong relational bonds.[2] These communities were small by necessity, yet they proved remarkably durable. Faith was not consumed as a product; it was lived as a way of life.

This household-based structure resists franchising logic. There was no centralized branding, no uniform worship experience, and no standardized leadership pipeline. Churches emerged organically within their social contexts, shaped by local culture while united by apostolic teaching.

Apostolic Oversight Without Uniformity

The early church did possess leadership and oversight, but not in the form of centralized control. Apostles provided doctrinal unity, relational accountability, and spiritual authority, yet local expressions varied widely. Paul's letters reveal churches wrestling with different issues—sexual ethics in Corinth, legalism in Galatia, persecution in Thessalonica. Apostolic guidance addressed context, not conformity.

Paul's missionary strategy further illustrates this point. He did not remain in one place to build a centralized institution. He planted communities, appointed elders, and entrusted leadership to local believers (Acts 14:23). His authority was relational and spiritual, not managerial. Paul did not franchise churches; he fathered them.

Alan Kreider argues that the early church's expansion was sustained not by centralized strategy, but by patient formation.[3]

Believers were shaped over time into distinctive communities whose lives bore witness to the gospel. Growth followed credibility, not cleverness.

Growth Through Witness, Not Attraction

Modern growth models often emphasize attraction—drawing people through programming, branding, or events. The early church grew primarily through witness. Believers embodied a way of life that provoked curiosity and conviction. Their commitment to mutual care, generosity, and holiness set them apart in a fractured world.

Acts 2:47 notes that the early believers enjoyed favor with the people, and "the Lord added to the church daily such as should be saved." The subject of the sentence is critical: the Lord added. Growth is attributed explicitly to divine action, not human strategy.

Rodney Stark's sociological analysis of early Christianity emphasizes that growth occurred through relational networks rather than mass persuasion.[4] Conversion spread through households, friendships, and social connections. Faith was transmitted through trust, not through spectacle.

This pattern challenges contemporary assumptions. Churches that prioritize attraction over formation may gather crowds quickly, but they often struggle to sustain depth. The early church prioritized formation, trusting God with increase.

Persecution as a Catalyst, Not a Crisis

One of the most overlooked aspects of early church growth is the role of persecution. Far from halting expansion, opposition often accelerated it. The scattering of believers following Stephen's martyrdom led to the spread of the gospel beyond Jerusalem (Acts 8:1–4). Growth emerged through displacement, not design.

This reality confronts modern growth paradigms that equate comfort with blessing. The early church did not expand because conditions were favorable, but because faith was resilient. Believers did not wait for ideal circumstances; they bore witness wherever they were scattered.

Tertullian famously observed that "the blood of the martyrs is the seed of the church."[5] This statement captures the paradox of early Christian growth: suffering produced fruit. Faithfulness under pressure authenticated the gospel in ways no program could.

Diversity Without Competition

The early church was remarkably diverse. Communities differed in ethnicity, language, socioeconomic status, and cultural practice. Jewish and Gentile believers navigated complex questions of identity and inclusion. Yet unity was maintained not through uniform practice, but through shared allegiance to Christ.

This diversity challenges competitive models of ministry. Churches were not vying for market share. They were cooperating within a shared mission. Paul's collection for the Jerusalem church (2 Corinthians 8–9) exemplifies this interdependence. Stronger churches supported weaker ones. Growth was communal, not competitive.

John Howard Yoder argues that the early church understood itself as a distinct social body, not an institution competing for influence.[6] Its power lay in its faithfulness, not in its dominance.

Why the Franchise Model Fails

When modern churches attempt to franchise growth, several problems emerge. Context is ignored. Relationships are reduced to processes. Leadership is measured by scalability rather than shepherding. Churches are pressured to conform to models that may not fit their calling or capacity.

Franchising assumes that success is transferable without loss. Scripture suggests otherwise. What God does in one place may not be what He does in another. Faithfulness is contextual. When pastors import strategies without discernment, they risk misalignment—and misalignment produces burden.

Research on congregational vitality consistently affirms that contextual responsiveness matters more than uniform programming.[7] Churches that honor local culture and relationships tend to sustain health more effectively than those that replicate external models wholesale.

Recovering the Early Church Vision

Recovering the early church vision does not mean abandoning structure, leadership, or planning. It means reordering priorities. Formation precedes expansion. Relationship precedes replication. Obedience precedes outcome.

The early church reminds us that growth is God's work, accomplished through faithful people living faithfully in their contexts. It was not fast, flashy, or frictionless. It was patient, costly, and deeply relational.

Implications for Today's Pastors

For pastors leading small or modest-sized churches, the early church offers both affirmation and challenge. Affirmation, because smallness does not disqualify faithfulness. Challenge, because depth requires intentional formation. The goal is not to remain small, but to remain obedient.

For pastors leading large churches, the early church offers caution. Scale must never outpace formation. Influence must never replace intimacy. Growth must never eclipse discipleship.

For all pastors, the early church offers freedom. Ministry is not a franchise to scale, but a calling to steward. Faithfulness, not uniform growth, remains the measure.

Growth Without Burden

When pastors stop treating Acts as a growth manual and begin receiving it as a testimony, the burden lifts. Growth returns to its rightful place as fruit rather than function. Churches are free to pursue health without comparison. Pastors are free to labor faithfully without anxiety.

The early church was not a franchise—and that is good news. It means that faithfulness still matters. It means that obedience still counts. It means that God is still responsible for the harvest.

The next chapter will explore how Jesus Himself prioritized depth over crowds, further dismantling assumptions about success and reinforcing the call to faithful discipleship.

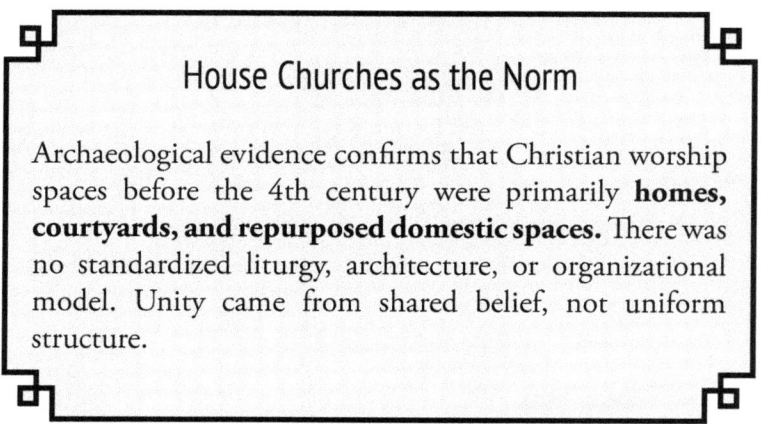

House Churches as the Norm

Archaeological evidence confirms that Christian worship spaces before the 4th century were primarily **homes, courtyards, and repurposed domestic spaces.** There was no standardized liturgy, architecture, or organizational model. Unity came from shared belief, not uniform structure.

Reflection Prayer

Living Christ,

Strip away the desire to imitate what You never assigned. Return me to the simplicity of devotion, teaching, prayer, and community. Help me resist the pressure to conform to models that distort my calling. Let my ministry reflect Your gospel, not a borrowed system.

Amen.

Chapter 6

Quality, Quantity, and the Way of Jesus

"Then said Jesus unto his disciples, If any man will come after me, let him deny himself, and take up his cross, and follow me."
— Matthew 16:24 (KJV)

The tension between quality and quantity is not a modern dilemma. It sits at the heart of the gospel narratives themselves. Long before churches debated attendance metrics and growth strategies, Jesus confronted a similar question: Is the goal to gather as many people as possible, or to form a people who truly follow?

Jesus never framed this tension as an either–or proposition, yet His ministry consistently revealed a clear priority. Crowds mattered to Him—but disciples mattered more. He welcomed the masses, healed the sick, fed the hungry, and preached to multitudes. Yet when it came time to entrust the future of His mission, He chose depth over breadth, formation over fascination, and obedience over enthusiasm.

This chapter explores that choice—and what it means for pastors today.

Crowds Were Common in Jesus' Ministry

The Gospels record numerous occasions when large crowds followed Jesus. People came from cities and villages, drawn by

His authority, compassion, and power. He healed publicly. He taught openly. He fed thousands with loaves and fish. From a distance, Jesus' ministry could easily be mistaken for a prototype of mass appeal.

Yet a closer reading reveals a striking pattern: Jesus never allowed crowds to define success.

In fact, the presence of crowds often became the setting for Jesus to clarify the cost of discipleship. Rather than lowering the bar to maintain momentum, He raised it. He spoke of self-denial, suffering, and allegiance that superseded family, comfort, and security (Luke 14:25–33). These teachings did not attract the casually interested; they sifted the committed.

Darrell Bock notes that Jesus' use of demanding language was intentional—designed to distinguish superficial enthusiasm from genuine commitment.[1] Jesus was not interested in accumulating admirers; He was forming followers.

When Jesus Thinned the Crowd

Few passages unsettle growth-driven assumptions more than John 6. After the feeding of the five thousand, Jesus experienced widespread popularity. The crowd followed Him eagerly, expecting more miracles and provision. Instead of meeting their expectations, Jesus confronted their motives. He spoke of Himself as the bread of life and called for a kind of belief that involved full allegiance.

The response was dramatic: *"From that time many of his disciples went back, and walked no more with him"* (John 6:66 KJV).

This moment deserves careful attention. Jesus had just experienced numerical success by any standard. Yet He did not attempt to preserve it. He did not soften His teaching or recalibrate His message. He allowed departure. And then He turned to the twelve—the small, committed core—and asked whether they too would leave.

From a modern perspective, this looks like failure. From a kingdom perspective, it reveals clarity. Jesus chose quality over quantity—not because quantity was unimportant, but because quality was foundational.

Dallas Willard famously argued that the greatest problem facing the church is not the lack of converts, but the lack of disciples.[2] John 6 illustrates this concern vividly. Jesus refused to confuse the two.

Discipleship as Formation, Not Information

Jesus' approach to discipleship was immersive and formative. He did not merely teach concepts; He invited people into a way of life. Disciples followed Him physically, observed His practices, absorbed His priorities, and learned obedience through relationship.

This kind of formation is inherently slow. It resists mass production. It requires proximity, patience, and presence. Formation cannot be rushed without being reduced.

The Sermon on the Mount provides a prime example. Jesus delivered it to a crowd, yet its content was anything but crowd-pleasing. He addressed heart-level obedience, internal righteousness, and costly love. The sermon did not function as a motivational speech; it functioned as a charter for a countercultural community.

N. T. Wright observes that Jesus' teaching consistently aimed at reshaping imagination and identity, not merely behavior.[3]

Such reshaping requires depth. It cannot be achieved through attendance alone.

Quantity Without Quality: A Recurrent Temptation

Scripture contains repeated warnings about quantity detached from faithfulness. Israel often struggled with this temptation. Numbers were counted. Armies were measured. Strength was assessed in terms of scale rather than obedience.

David's census in 2 Samuel 24 offers a sobering example. By counting Israel's fighting men, David sought reassurance in numbers rather than trust in God. The act was interpreted as a failure of faith, resulting in judgment. The issue was not counting per se, but misplaced confidence.

The prophets repeatedly confronted Israel for pursuing outward strength while neglecting inward fidelity. Amos warned of religious activity without justice. Isaiah condemned worship divorced from obedience. In each case, quantity of religious expression masked a lack of covenant faithfulness.

Walter Brueggemann notes that prophetic critique consistently exposes the danger of equating visible success with divine approval.[4] This pattern carries directly into New Testament ecclesiology.

The Early Church and the Priority of Depth

The early church experienced periods of numerical growth, particularly in Jerusalem. Yet even there, growth was anchored in devotion: "They continued steadfastly in the apostles' doctrine and fellowship, and in breaking of bread, and in prayers" (Acts 2:42 KJV). Luke presents devotion as the foundation; growth follows as a result.

As the church spread, depth remained essential. Paul's letters reveal a deep concern for formation—spiritual maturity, doctrinal stability, and ethical transformation. He labored intensely to "present every man perfect in Christ Jesus" (Colossians 1:28 KJV). This goal required instruction, correction, and patience.

Alan Kreider emphasizes that early Christian growth was sustained because communities were formed deeply before they multiplied widely.[5] Without such formation, persecution would have extinguished the movement. Depth created resilience.

Pastoral Ministry and the Pressure to Produce

Modern pastors often inherit a subtle pressure to prioritize quantity. Attendance is visible. Depth is harder to measure. Growth can be charted. Formation unfolds quietly over time. In systems that reward what can be counted, pastors may feel compelled to emphasize numerical outcomes even when doing so undermines long-term health.

This pressure affects preaching, programming, and pastoral priorities. Sermons may become motivational rather than formative. Programs may be designed for appeal rather than transformation. Discipleship may be reduced to content delivery rather than life-on-life formation.

Research on church vitality suggests that congregations focused primarily on attraction often struggle with retention and depth.[6] Growth that outpaces formation produces instability. Churches may expand quickly only to contract just as rapidly when enthusiasm fades.

Jesus' Metric: Obedience

When Jesus defined fruitfulness, He consistently pointed to obedience. "If ye love me, keep my commandments" (John

14:15 KJV). Love is measured not by intensity of feeling or size of following, but by faithfulness of response.

In the Great Commission, Jesus commanded His disciples not merely to make converts, but to make disciples—"teaching them to observe all things whatsoever I have commanded you" (Matthew 28:20 KJV). Teaching obedience, not merely belief, was central to His vision.

This emphasis reframes growth. Numerical increase without obedience is incomplete. Depth of obedience—even in small numbers—is fully aligned with Christ's mission.

The Cost of Choosing Depth

Choosing quality over quantity carries cost. It may mean slower growth. It may mean smaller crowds. It may mean misunderstanding by those who equate success with scale. Jesus accepted these costs without hesitation.

Bonhoeffer described discipleship as costly grace—grace that demands obedience and transforms life.[7] Cheap grace, by contrast, offers belonging without transformation. Churches that prioritize quantity often drift toward cheap grace—not intentionally, but pragmatically.

The pastoral challenge is to resist this drift. Faithfulness requires courage to disappoint expectations in order to remain obedient.

Quality Produces a Different Kind of Growth

Quality-focused ministry does produce growth—but often of a different kind. Leaders are developed. Faith matures. Communities deepen. Witness becomes credible. Over time, numerical growth may follow, but it does so organically rather than forcefully.

James Dunn observes that early Christian communities grew because their transformed lives were compelling.[8] Growth emerged from credibility, not campaigns.

This kind of growth cannot be engineered. It must be cultivated. Pastors who commit to depth trust God with increase.

Reframing the Question

The critical question is not How many are we gathering? but Who are we forming? When pastors shift the question, priorities realign. Sermons deepen. Discipleship strengthens. Shepherding regains prominence.

Quantity is not dismissed; it is reordered. It becomes fruit, not fuel.

The Freedom of Jesus' Way

Jesus' way is liberating precisely because it clarifies responsibility. Pastors are responsible to teach, shepherd, and model obedience. They are not responsible to guarantee outcomes. When quality becomes the priority, growth loses its power to burden.

The way of Jesus is narrow, but it is light. It demands faithfulness, not frenzy. It calls for depth, not display.

The next chapter will examine growth tools often overlooked by small-church pastors, showing how depth-oriented ministry can be practiced intentionally without pressure to perform.

Catechesis Before Conversion

In the early church, converts often underwent **months or years of catechesis** before baptism. This slow process prioritized depth, repentance, and doctrinal understanding. Modern altar-call culture would have been foreign to early Christian formation practices.

Reflection Prayer

Patient Teacher,

Teach me to value depth over speed and formation over applause. Deliver me from impatience that confuses fruit with numbers. Help me disciple faithfully, even when progress feels slow. Shape my heart to desire what produces lasting fruit.

Amen.

Chapter 7

Growth Tools Small Churches Often Overlook

"So the churches were strengthened in the faith, and increased in number daily."

— Acts 16:5 (KJV)

When pastors think about growth tools, the conversation often turns quickly to what they lack—staff, budgets, facilities, technology, or visibility. Small churches are frequently framed in terms of deficit. What is rarely acknowledged is that small churches possess tools that large churches often struggle to recover once scale increases. These tools are not flashy. They do not lend themselves easily to conferences or templates. Yet they are profoundly biblical, deeply effective, and well-suited for forming mature disciples.

This chapter argues that many small churches already have what they need to grow faithfully. What is often missing is not capacity, but confidence—confidence to value tools that Scripture affirms but modern ministry culture tends to overlook.

Proximity as a Discipleship Tool

One of the most underappreciated assets of small churches is proximity. Pastors are accessible. Leaders are known. Members are not anonymous. This closeness is not a limitation; it is a formative environment.

Jesus formed disciples through proximity. He lived with them, walked with them, ate with them, and allowed them to observe His life closely. Discipleship in the Gospels is not classroom-based alone; it is life-shared. The power of Jesus' teaching was inseparable from the intimacy of His presence.

Small churches are uniquely positioned to practice this kind of formation. Pastors can know the spiritual condition of their people. They can tailor care rather than generalize it. Correction and encouragement can occur within trusted relationships rather than institutional processes.

Dallas Willard emphasizes that discipleship requires intentional environments where people learn to live as apprentices of Jesus.[1] Proximity makes such environments possible. Large systems often attempt to simulate intimacy through programs; small churches possess it organically.

Pastoral Accessibility as a Strength

In many large congregations, pastoral care is necessarily delegated. In small churches, it remains personal. Pastors visit hospitals, attend family milestones, and walk with people through crises. These moments may not increase attendance immediately, but they deepen trust and credibility.

Scripture consistently affirms shepherding as relational work. Peter exhorts elders to "feed the flock of God which is among you" (1 Peter 5:2 KJV). The phrase among you implies presence. Shepherds are not distant overseers; they are embedded caregivers.

Sociological studies confirm that pastoral presence significantly impacts congregational health. Nancy Ammerman notes that smaller congregations often demonstrate higher levels of relational satisfaction precisely because leaders are accessible and involved.[2] This accessibility fosters resilience and long-term commitment— forms of growth that do not always register numerically.

Leadership Development Through Relationship

Small churches often underestimate their capacity to develop leaders. Without formal pipelines or extensive training programs, pastors may assume leadership development is beyond their reach. In reality, relational environments are ideal for mentoring.

Jesus developed leaders by inviting participation. He sent the disciples out two by two, debriefed their experiences, corrected misunderstandings, and entrusted increasing responsibility over time (Luke 10:1–20). Leadership formation was gradual and relational.

Paul adopted a similar approach. He traveled with companions, mentored younger leaders, and entrusted local leadership to elders within each community (Acts 14:23). Timothy's development occurred within the context of close relationship and shared ministry.

Research on leadership formation consistently affirms that mentoring relationships are among the most effective means of developing mature leaders.[3] Small churches, precisely because of their size, can offer this kind of personalized formation more readily than large systems.

Community Embeddedness

Small churches are often deeply woven into the fabric of their communities. Members live nearby. Relationships extend beyond

Sunday gatherings. The church is known—not as a destination, but as a presence.

This embeddedness is a powerful growth tool. The early church expanded through relational networks rather than public campaigns. Believers lived visibly different lives within their communities, provoking questions and curiosity (Acts 2:47).

Rodney Stark's analysis of early Christian growth highlights the role of everyday relationships in spreading faith.[4] Conversion occurred through trust—family, friendship, and neighborly connection. Small churches, by virtue of their proximity, are well-positioned for this kind of witness.

Growth that emerges from community credibility tends to be slower but more durable. It reflects trust earned over time rather than attraction generated by novelty.

Teaching Depth Over Breadth

Small churches have the freedom to teach patiently. Sermons and studies can build cumulatively rather than episodically. Pastors can revisit themes, address questions, and ensure understanding.

The New Testament places significant emphasis on teaching. The early believers devoted themselves to the apostles' doctrine (Acts 2:42). Paul instructed Timothy to guard sound teaching and to entrust it to faithful people who could teach others (2 Timothy 2:2). Depth was prioritized over speed.

Gordon Fee notes that Paul's vision for teaching aimed at shaping worldview and character, not merely conveying information.[5] This kind of formation requires time and continuity—conditions more readily available in small congregations.

Accountability and Mutual Care

Small churches often practice accountability informally, through relationship rather than policy. Members notice when someone is absent. Needs are recognized quickly. Care is shared.

Scripture presents the Church as a body where members care for one another (1 Corinthians 12:25–26). This mutuality is difficult to cultivate at scale without intentional systems. In small churches, it can emerge naturally.

Christian Schwarz's research on church health identifies loving relationships as a key indicator of vitality.[6] Churches that foster genuine care tend to sustain engagement even when growth is modest.

Prayer as Central Practice

Prayer is often cited as essential, yet easily marginalized when programs multiply. Small churches can center prayer without competing demands. Prayer meetings can be intimate, participatory, and formative.

The early church prayed frequently and collectively (Acts 4:23–31). Prayer was not an add-on; it was a lifeline. Decisions, crises, and mission were all shaped through prayerful discernment.

Walter Brueggemann argues that prayer reorients communities toward dependence rather than control.[7] When prayer is central, growth is received as gift rather than manufactured result.

Flexibility and Responsiveness

Small churches can adapt quickly. Decisions are made relationally. Change does not require navigating complex bureaucracy. This flexibility allows churches to respond to real needs rather than maintaining rigid structures.

In Acts 15, the Jerusalem council models communal discernment—listening, debating, and responding to emerging challenges. The process is relational and Spirit-led rather than procedural.

Flexibility does not mean lack of order; it means responsiveness guided by wisdom. Small churches can pivot without losing identity, a significant advantage in changing cultural contexts.

Measuring What Matters

One reason small churches undervalue their tools is the dominance of numerical metrics. Attendance and budgets are easy to count; formation and faithfulness are not. Yet Scripture consistently prioritizes what cannot be easily measured.

Paul speaks of growth in terms of love, maturity, and unity (Ephesians 4:13–16). These indicators require discernment rather than calculation. They invite pastors to observe lives rather than charts.

Reframing metrics frees pastors to celebrate progress that might otherwise go unnoticed—restored relationships, growing prayerfulness, emerging leaders, and deepening commitment.

Integrating Tools Without Pressure

The tools described in this chapter are not techniques to manipulate outcomes. They are practices to cultivate health. When employed faithfully, they create conditions in which growth—of various kinds—can emerge.

Small churches do not need to become large to be effective. They need to be intentional. Growth tools rooted in proximity, relationship, teaching, prayer, and community presence align closely with the way of Jesus and the witness of the early church.

Confidence in God's Design

This chapter invites pastors to reassess what they already possess. Smallness is not an obstacle to growth; it is a context for it. When pastors value the tools inherent in their setting, they are freed from striving to imitate models that do not fit.

The goal is not to remain small, but to remain faithful. Growth that flows from faithfulness may look different from what is expected, but it will be sustainable and aligned with God's purposes.

The next chapter will address when growth goes wrong—examining what happens when expansion outpaces formation and why discernment is essential for long-term health.

Relational Leadership in the Patristic Era

Church fathers like Ignatius of Antioch emphasized proximity between bishop and congregation. Leadership was relational, not distant. Shepherding occurred through presence, correspondence, and shared suffering—not administrative hierarchy.

Reflection Prayer

God who works through presence,

Open my eyes to the gifts already among us. Help me steward proximity, relationship, and prayer with faith. Teach me to see power in simplicity and strength in faithfulness. Let me use what I have, trusting You with the rest.

Amen.

Chapter 8

When Growth Goes Wrong

"And he spake also a parable unto them; No man putteth a piece of a new garment upon an old; if otherwise, then both the new maketh a rent, and the piece that was taken out of the new agreeth not with the old."

— Luke 5:36 (KJV)

Growth is not inherently good.

It is only good when it is rightly ordered.

This statement may sound counterintuitive in a ministry culture that celebrates expansion almost without qualification. Yet Scripture, history, and lived pastoral experience all testify to the same truth: growth that is not aligned with maturity eventually becomes destructive. When increase outruns integrity, when expansion outpaces formation, and when visibility exceeds capacity, growth no longer blesses—it burdens.

This chapter explores what happens when growth goes wrong—not to discourage pastors from desiring increase, but to warn them against pursuing it without discernment. Many of the deepest wounds in pastoral ministry are not caused by lack of growth, but by growth that arrived before a church was prepared to steward it.

Growth Without Infrastructure

One of the most common ways growth goes wrong is when numerical increase outpaces organizational and relational infrastructure. Churches experience sudden influx—new attendees, new members, new expectations—without the systems, leadership, or clarity necessary to support them.

The book of Acts provides a striking example. In Acts 6, rapid growth in Jerusalem led to internal tension. The complaint of neglected widows revealed a structural weakness. The apostles did not deny the blessing of growth, but neither did they ignore its strain. They responded by reorganizing leadership, appointing servants to ensure care, and protecting their primary calling to prayer and the ministry of the Word.

This moment is instructive. Growth created pressure, and pressure exposed weakness. The apostles did not spiritualize the problem away. They addressed it structurally and relationally. Growth was stewarded, not simply celebrated.

Modern churches often skip this step. Excited by attendance increases, leaders delay necessary adjustments. They assume momentum will solve problems that actually require maturity. When systems lag behind scale, people suffer—and pastors carry the weight.

Leadership That Is Unready

Growth can also go wrong when leadership development lags behind numerical expansion. Churches may gain people faster than they can form leaders. Volunteers are promoted prematurely. Authority is given without accountability. Responsibilities multiply without preparation.

Scripture consistently emphasizes the character and maturity of leaders. Paul's qualifications for elders and deacons in 1 Timothy 3 and Titus 1 are deeply relational and ethical. Leadership is not granted based on enthusiasm alone, but on tested faithfulness.

Robert Clinton's research on leadership development highlights the dangers of *role overload*—placing individuals in positions they are not yet prepared to sustain.[1] When leaders are stretched beyond capacity, burnout follows. Churches experience instability not because they grew, but because growth was entrusted to unformed leadership.

Pastors often feel responsible for holding everything together during such seasons. The burden intensifies as growth reveals gaps that cannot be filled quickly or easily.

Crowds Without Disciples

Perhaps the most serious danger of misordered growth is the creation of crowds without disciples. Attendance increases, but formation stagnates. People participate, but they are not transformed. Belonging replaces obedience.

Jesus warned explicitly against this outcome. In Matthew 7, He spoke of those who performed religious acts yet did not know Him. Their activity was impressive; their relationship was absent. The danger was not smallness, but superficiality.

Dallas Willard famously argued that the church's central failure is the absence of intentional discipleship.[2] Growth that prioritizes attraction over formation exacerbates this failure. People are gathered faster than they can be shaped. Churches become wide and shallow—impressive from a distance, fragile up close.

This kind of growth places enormous strain on pastors. Shepherding a large group of spiritually immature believers requires constant crisis management. The burden increases because depth was sacrificed for speed.

Moral and Doctrinal Compromise

Growth can also go wrong when leaders compromise moral or doctrinal integrity to maintain momentum. Teachings are softened to avoid offense. Accountability is relaxed to preserve numbers. Truth becomes negotiable.

The letters to the churches in Revelation address this danger directly. Pergamum and Thyatira were rebuked not for lack of activity, but for tolerating false teaching and moral compromise (Revelation 2:14–15, 20). Growth or influence did not excuse deviation. Jesus' concern was fidelity, not popularity.

Dietrich Bonhoeffer warned that when the Church abandons costly obedience, it exchanges discipleship for accommodation.[3] Churches may grow numerically under such conditions, but the growth corrodes spiritual integrity. Pastors who participate in or permit such compromise often carry deep internal conflict—the burden of success purchased at the expense of faithfulness.

Financial Expansion Without Stewardship

Financial growth is often celebrated as a sign of blessing, yet it carries its own dangers. Increased resources require increased accountability. Without clear stewardship, transparency, and discipline, financial growth can lead to misuse, mistrust, and moral failure.

The New Testament consistently treats resources as trust, not entitlement. Paul was meticulous in handling financial gifts, ensuring accountability and integrity (2 Corinthians 8:20–21). He understood that growth in resources required growth in responsibility.

Churches that grow financially without corresponding stewardship structures place immense pressure on leaders. The burden of managing expectations, funding expansion, and maintaining trust can overshadow the spiritual work of ministry.

Visibility Without Accountability

As churches grow, visibility increases. Leaders become more public. Influence expands. Without accountability, this visibility can become dangerous.

Scripture consistently warns that leadership requires oversight. Even apostles were accountable to one another (Galatians 2:11–14). Isolation breeds vulnerability. Growth that elevates leaders without embedding them in accountable relationships creates conditions ripe for failure.

Research on pastoral failure consistently identifies isolation as a major contributing factor.[4] When leaders lack trusted relationships that speak truth and offer correction, growth amplifies weaknesses rather than maturing strengths.

Growth That Outpaces the Soul

Perhaps the most painful way growth goes wrong is when it outpaces the pastor's own spiritual health. Ministry demands increase. Time for prayer decreases. Visibility grows. Intimacy with God erodes. The pastor becomes the engine of growth rather than a recipient of grace.

Jesus consistently withdrew to pray, even at the height of public demand (Mark 1:35). He modeled rhythms that protected the soul. Growth did not excuse neglect of communion with the Father.

Eugene Peterson warned against pastors becoming "shopkeepers" rather than shepherds—busy managing religious goods while neglecting their own spiritual formation.[5] Growth that is not accompanied by soul care eventually becomes unsustainable.

The Emotional Toll on Congregations

When growth goes wrong, congregations suffer alongside leaders. People feel overlooked. Relationships strain. Long-term members feel displaced. Newcomers feel disconnected. The sense of family erodes.

Sociological studies indicate that rapid congregational growth often disrupts relational cohesion.[6] Without intentional integration, churches fragment into subgroups. The very growth celebrated publicly produces quiet grief privately.

Pastors absorb this tension. They mediate conflicts, manage expectations, and attempt to hold community together while momentum pushes forward. The burden becomes heavy because growth was not paced.

Scripture's Call to Discernment

Scripture does not reject growth; it insists on discernment. Jesus' parables repeatedly emphasize readiness—new wine requires new wineskins (Luke 5:37–38). Timing matters. Capacity matters. Alignment matters.

The wisdom literature reinforces this principle. Proverbs cautions against haste and presumption. Ecclesiastes reminds us that there is a season for everything. Growth outside its season becomes destructive.

Discernment asks not Can we grow? but Should we grow now—and how?

Reordering Growth as Stewardship

When growth is understood as stewardship rather than achievement, its dangers are mitigated. Pastors prepare infrastructure before expansion. They develop leaders before delegating authority. They deepen formation before widening reach.

This reordering requires courage. It may mean slowing momentum. It may mean disappointing expectations. It may mean saying no to opportunities that exceed capacity. Yet such restraint reflects wisdom, not fear.

James reminds believers that wisdom is "first pure, then peaceable, gentle, and easy to be entreated" (James 3:17). Growth that reflects wisdom builds peace rather than pressure.

Freedom Through Rightly Ordered Growth

This chapter is not a warning against growth; it is an invitation to freedom. Pastors are not required to chase increase at the expense of health. They are called to steward what God entrusts, when He entrusts it.

When growth goes wrong, the burden becomes unbearable. When growth is rightly ordered, it becomes a joy.

The next chapter will address church shenanigans to avoid—the subtle practices and habits that undermine health even when intentions are good—further equipping pastors to lead faithfully without falling into unnecessary traps.

The Medieval Church and Institutional Overgrowth

By the Middle Ages, the Church wielded immense power and wealth. Growth outpaced spiritual reform, leading to corruption, abuse, and public distrust. The Protestant Reformation was, in part, a response to **unchecked institutional growth without accountability.**

Reflection Prayer

Wise Counselor,

Give me discernment to recognize growth that is outpacing grace. Protect my heart from pride, fear, and exhaustion. Teach me to pause when needed and to pace growth with wisdom. May expansion never cost integrity, intimacy, or obedience.

Amen.

Chapter 9
Church Shenanigans to Avoid

"Be not conformed to this world: but be ye transformed by the renewing of your mind."
— Romans 12:2 (KJV)

Not every threat to a church's health arrives dressed as rebellion, immorality, or doctrinal error. Some of the most damaging practices wear the clothing of good intentions. They are rarely labeled as sin. They are often applauded as innovation, relevance, or strategic thinking. Yet over time, they hollow out faithfulness, distort calling, and exhaust pastors.

This chapter addresses what many pastors privately recognize but rarely name openly—church shenanigans. By this, I do not mean malicious schemes or deliberate misconduct. I mean the quiet habits, borrowed assumptions, and unexamined practices that feel normal in modern ministry culture but are misaligned with Scripture and destructive to long-term health.

These shenanigans rarely cause immediate collapse. They erode slowly. And because they are common, they often go unchallenged.

Borrowed Vision Without Discernment

One of the most prevalent shenanigans in contemporary ministry is borrowed vision. Pastors attend conferences, read books, or watch successful churches online and begin to import language, goals, and strategies wholesale—often without discerning whether they fit their context or calling.

Vision is meant to be received, not replicated. Scripture presents vision as a response to God's specific assignment, not as a template transferable across settings. Moses' vision was not Joshua's. David's was not Solomon's. Paul's apostolic calling differed sharply from Peter's pastoral focus.

When pastors borrow vision without discernment, they subtly abandon stewardship of the church they have been given. Expectations rise that cannot be met. Language changes that people do not recognize. Congregations begin to feel as though their identity has been replaced rather than refined.

Andy Crouch warns that leadership divorced from place and people becomes abstract and coercive.[1] Vision must emerge from proximity, prayer, and discernment—not comparison.

Chasing Trends Instead of Truth

Trends move faster than formation. Ministry culture cycles through emphases—branding, online engagement, worship styles, leadership models—often with little theological reflection. Churches feel pressure to keep up lest they appear outdated or irrelevant.

The danger is not innovation itself, but imitation without discernment. Scripture calls the Church to faithfulness, not fashion. The apostle Paul urged Timothy to guard what had been entrusted to him, not to chase novelty (1 Timothy 6:20).

Karl Barth famously cautioned pastors to preach with the Bible in one hand and the newspaper in the other—but never to confuse which hand carries authority.[2] When trends begin to shape theology rather than theology shaping practice, pastors find themselves reactive rather than rooted.

Trends promise quick impact. Faithfulness requires patient obedience.

Measuring What Is Easy Instead of What Is True

Churches often measure what is easiest to count rather than what matters most. Attendance, giving, and engagement are visible and quantifiable. Love, maturity, repentance, and obedience are not.

When easy metrics dominate evaluation, ministry priorities shift. Programs are optimized for participation rather than formation. Sermons are shaped for appeal rather than truth. Discipleship is reduced to content consumption.

Scripture consistently resists this reduction. Paul prays for churches to grow in love, knowledge of God, and spiritual discernment (Philippians 1:9–11). These qualities require observation, not spreadsheets.

Christian Schwarz's research affirms that churches grow healthiest when they prioritize qualitative factors—relationships, spiritual vitality, leadership development—over numerical targets.[3] Measuring the wrong things produces the wrong outcomes.

Performance-Driven Ministry

Another common shenanigan is performance-driven ministry. Services become productions. Leaders feel pressure to deliver excellence every week. Authenticity is replaced by polish.

Excellence is not inherently wrong. Scripture calls believers to offer their best to God. The problem arises when performance becomes a substitute for presence—when pastors feel valued more for how well they perform than for who they are.

Jesus consistently resisted performative spirituality. He warned against practicing righteousness to be seen by others (Matthew 6:1). He withdrew from crowds rather than cultivating spectacle. His authority flowed from authenticity, not theatrics.

Eugene Peterson lamented the transformation of pastors into "religious professionals" who manage appearances rather than shepherd souls.[4] Performance-driven ministry may impress people, but it often isolates leaders and erodes integrity.

Copying Systems Without Capacity

Systems designed for large churches often collapse small ones. Complex organizational structures, extensive programming, and multi-layered leadership models may function well at scale but overwhelm smaller congregations.

When pastors import systems without considering capacity, they create frustration. Volunteers burn out. Resources stretch thin. Energy is diverted from core practices—prayer, teaching, care—toward maintenance of machinery.

Scripture emphasizes wisdom and order, but it also values proportion. Jesus' parable of the tower-builder warns against beginning what cannot be finished (Luke 14:28–30). Capacity matters. Faithfulness includes restraint.

Research on congregational vitality indicates that alignment between structure and size is essential for sustainability.[5] Systems must serve people, not the other way around.

Neglecting Formation for Visibility

Visibility can be intoxicating. Social media, livestreams, and online platforms offer unprecedented reach. Churches can appear larger and more influential than ever before. Yet visibility without formation is hollow.

When energy is invested primarily in outward presence, inward formation often suffers. Prayer meetings dwindle. Teaching is shortened. Shepherding becomes reactive. Over time, the church becomes known more for its presence than its depth.

The early church prioritized formation long before visibility. They devoted themselves to teaching, fellowship, breaking of bread, and prayer (Acts 2:42). Their witness flowed from their way of life, not their platform.

James K. A. Smith argues that Christian formation is shaped by practices, not merely messages.[6] Churches that neglect formative practices in pursuit of visibility risk producing consumers rather than disciples.

Avoiding Hard Conversations

Another subtle shenanigan is conflict avoidance. In the name of peace or growth, pastors may avoid addressing sin, dysfunction, or unhealthy patterns. Problems are deferred rather than confronted.

Scripture consistently calls leaders to speak truth in love (Ephesians 4:15). Love does not ignore sin; it seeks restoration. Churches that avoid hard conversations often experience greater conflict later, when issues have deepened.

The letters to the churches in Revelation reveal Christ's willingness to confront. His rebukes are specific, direct, and restorative. Avoidance is not pastoral; it is permissive.

Research on organizational health confirms that unresolved conflict undermines trust and morale.[7] Pastors who avoid hard conversations often carry heavier emotional burdens over time.

Confusing Activity with Fruitfulness

Busy churches are not necessarily healthy churches. Activity can mask emptiness. Calendars fill. Programs multiply. Leaders stay exhausted.

Scripture distinguishes fruit from activity. Jesus cursed the fig tree not because it had no leaves, but because it had no fruit (Mark 11:12–14). Leaves create appearance; fruit reveals substance.

Pastors often feel pressure to keep churches busy. Yet busyness without formation exhausts people and leaders alike. Fruitfulness flows from abiding, not activity (John 15:4–5).

Treating Growth as Proof of God's Favor

Perhaps the most dangerous shenanigan is theological: treating growth as evidence of divine approval. This assumption places unbearable pressure on pastors and distorts the gospel.

Scripture offers no such equation. Faithfulness and suffering often coexist. Jesus Himself was rejected. The prophets were marginalized. The apostles endured persecution.

Walter Brueggemann notes that equating success with blessing reflects a theology of triumph rather than a theology of covenant faithfulness.[8] When growth becomes proof of favor, decline becomes proof of failure—an assumption Scripture does not support.

Naming Shenanigans Without Shame

This chapter is not written to accuse pastors, but to free them. Many of these shenanigans are adopted unintentionally. They are learned through immersion in ministry culture rather than deliberate rebellion.

Freedom begins with naming. Once practices are named, they can be examined, corrected, or released. Pastors are not required to carry cultural expectations that conflict with Scripture.

The goal is not to reject all innovation or structure, but to submit every practice to biblical discernment.

Returning to Simplicity

The antidote to church shenanigans is not cynicism; it is simplicity. Returning to prayer, teaching, shepherding, accountability, and obedience re-centers ministry around what Scripture affirms.

Simplicity does not mean lack of excellence. It means clarity of purpose. It means knowing why we do what we do—and who we are doing it for.

When pastors resist shenanigans, they reclaim joy. The burden lifts. Faithfulness feels light again.

The next chapter will explore how growth must always be contextual, affirming that faithfulness looks different in different places—and that God's work cannot be reduced to a single model.

Indulgences and Performance Religion

In the late medieval period, indulgences were sold as spiritual shortcuts. This practice illustrates how **performance-based spirituality** replaces formation when growth and revenue become primary goals. Reformers challenged these "religious shenanigans" with a return to Scripture and obedience.

Reflection Prayer

Holy God,

Expose practices I have accepted without examining. Deliver me from trends that replace truth and performance that replaces presence. Purify my leadership motives and restore simplicity to my service. Let my ministry be shaped by Scripture and guided by Your Spirit.

Amen.

Chapter 10
Healthy Growth Is Contextual

"To every thing there is a season, and a time to every purpose
under the heaven."
— Ecclesiastes 3:1 (KJV)

One of the most persistent mistakes in modern ministry is the belief that healthy growth can be standardized. Conferences package it. Books systematize it. Metrics promise to measure it. The underlying assumption is simple and seductive: If a model works there, it should work here.

Scripture resists this assumption at every turn.

Healthy growth in the Church has never been uniform, predictable, or easily transferable. It is contextual—shaped by geography, culture, people, history, resources, leadership, and season. When pastors ignore context, growth becomes forced. When they honor it, growth becomes faithful.

This chapter argues that discernment of context is not optional for pastoral leadership; it is essential. Growth that ignores context may expand briefly, but it rarely endures.

God Works Through Place

The biblical story is deeply rooted in place. God calls Abram to leave one land and journey to another. Israel's covenant life is shaped by geography—desert, land, exile, and return. Jesus' ministry unfolds in specific towns and regions, each carrying its own social and religious dynamics.

The incarnation itself affirms contextuality. God does not save humanity from a distance; He enters a particular culture, speaks a particular language, and lives within a particular community. The gospel is universal in scope, but always local in expression.

Missiologists have long noted that Christianity spreads most faithfully when it takes root in local soil rather than remaining an imported form.[1] When churches attempt to replicate models developed elsewhere without contextual adaptation, they risk appearing foreign, disconnected, or imposed.

Healthy growth honors place.

The New Testament and Contextual Churches

The letters of the New Testament reveal churches shaped by their environments. Corinth struggled with moral permissiveness. Galatia wrestled with legalism. Thessalonica endured persecution. Philippi demonstrated generosity amid poverty. Each church required specific pastoral counsel.

Paul did not send identical letters to every congregation. He addressed concrete situations. He contextualized application while maintaining doctrinal consistency. Unity was theological; expression was local.

This pattern undermines the notion of a universal growth strategy. The same gospel produced different challenges and outcomes in different places. Growth was not measured against another church's experience, but against faithfulness within each context.

Gordon Fee emphasizes that Paul's pastoral theology was deeply situational, responding to lived realities rather than abstract ideals.[2] Healthy growth, therefore, cannot be abstracted from context without distortion.

Seasons Matter

Context is not static. Churches pass through seasons—planting, stabilizing, expanding, pruning, rebuilding. Ecclesiastes reminds us that timing is as important as action. What is wise in one season may be destructive in another.

Many pastoral burdens arise from trying to live in the wrong season. Churches in recovery attempt expansion too soon. Congregations in decline resist necessary pruning. Young churches pursue complexity prematurely. Mature churches cling to methods suited to an earlier era.

Jesus' parables repeatedly emphasize readiness and timing. Seeds grow according to seasons. Harvest follows sowing. New wine requires new wineskins. Wisdom discerns when as carefully as what.

Pastors who ignore seasonality often misinterpret resistance as failure, when it may be invitation to wait, tend, or redirect.

People Shape Growth

Churches are not abstract entities; they are communities of people with histories, wounds, gifts, and limitations. Healthy growth must account for who is present, not merely who is desired.

The early church did not grow by replacing people, but by forming them. Leaders worked with the communities they had, developing maturity over time. When pastors chase growth by attempting to attract a different demographic rather than shepherding their current flock, relational trust erodes.

Sociological studies of congregational vitality consistently show that churches grow healthiest when they align vision with the actual capacities and commitments of their members.[3] Growth imposed without regard for people's readiness produces resistance and fatigue.

Healthy growth is humane.

Resources and Realism

Context includes resources—financial, relational, and organizational. Scripture commends stewardship, not presumption. Jesus' warning about building a tower without counting the cost underscores the importance of realism (Luke 14:28–30).

Churches often experience strain when vision exceeds capacity. Leaders may feel compelled to "act in faith" by expanding without provision. Scripture, however, distinguishes faith from folly. Faith trusts God; folly ignores wisdom.

Financial growth, staff expansion, and program development must be paced according to provision and readiness. Growth that outruns resources places unsustainable pressure on leaders and congregations.

Research on nonprofit sustainability confirms that organizations that expand faster than their resource base experience higher rates of burnout and collapse.[4] The Church is not exempt from these realities.

Leadership Capacity and Calling

Context also includes the pastor's own calling and capacity. Not every leader is wired for the same kind of growth. Some excel at pioneering; others at pastoring. Some thrive in complexity; others in intimacy. Scripture affirms diversity of gifts and roles.

When pastors pursue growth styles misaligned with their calling, ministry becomes heavy. Leaders feel forced to perform outside their grace. Over time, discouragement and burnout follow.

The apostle Paul understood his calling clearly. He described himself as a wise master builder who laid foundations, while others built upon them (1 Corinthians 3:10). He did not attempt to do every kind of work. He honored the diversity of roles within God's economy.

Healthy growth aligns with calling rather than contradicting it.

Cultural Shifts and Adaptation

Context includes culture—and culture changes. Churches that once thrived in a particular social environment may find that methods effective in one era lose resonance in another. Adaptation becomes necessary, but adaptation must be discerned, not reactive.

The early church navigated significant cultural transitions as the gospel moved from Jewish to Gentile contexts. Acts 15 records a moment of communal discernment, where leaders adjusted practice without compromising doctrine. Cultural sensitivity was exercised in service of unity and mission.

Missional theologians emphasize that faithful adaptation requires listening—listening to Scripture, the Spirit, and the surrounding culture.[5] Churches that refuse to adapt risk irrelevance; churches that adapt without discernment risk compromise.

Healthy growth navigates this tension with humility and wisdom.

Metrics Must Fit the Mission

Contextual growth requires contextual metrics. What counts as progress in one church may not apply in another. A rural congregation may measure growth through community impact and longevity. An urban church may track small-group participation and leadership development. A church in a hostile environment may celebrate perseverance rather than expansion.

Paul prayed for churches to grow in love, knowledge, and discernment (Philippians 1:9–11). These qualities resist easy measurement. Yet they remain essential indicators of health.

When pastors borrow metrics from contexts unlike their own, discouragement follows. Contextual metrics restore joy by aligning expectations with reality.

Discernment Over Duplication

The temptation to duplicate successful models is understandable. Duplication promises certainty. Discernment requires patience. Yet Scripture consistently elevates discernment.

Romans 12 calls believers to discern the will of God rather than conform to prevailing patterns. Discernment asks different questions: What is God doing here? What is He asking of us now? What faithfulness looks like in this place and time?

Walter Brueggemann argues that discernment resists empire-like standardization by honoring God's freedom to act differently in different contexts.[6] The Church bears witness not by uniformity, but by faithfulness embodied locally.

Growth That Fits

When growth fits its context, it blesses rather than burdens. Leaders feel aligned rather than strained. Congregations move together rather than being dragged forward. Expansion, when it occurs, feels organic rather than forced.

This does not mean growth will always be comfortable. Faithfulness often stretches capacity. But it stretches within grace, not against it.

Freedom Through Contextual Faithfulness

This chapter offers pastors freedom: freedom to stop comparing, freedom to stop copying, freedom to stop carrying expectations God never assigned. Contextual faithfulness restores joy to ministry.

Healthy growth is not measured by how closely a church resembles another, but by how faithfully it embodies the gospel where it is planted.

The next chapter will explore the development of pastoral leadership over time—moving from pastor to shepherd to spiritual father—and how leadership maturity shapes sustainable growth.

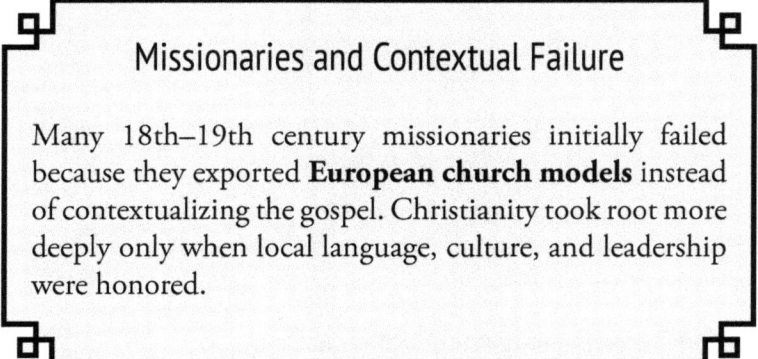

Missionaries and Contextual Failure

Many 18th–19th century missionaries initially failed because they exported **European church models** instead of contextualizing the gospel. Christianity took root more deeply only when local language, culture, and leadership were honored.

Reflection Prayer

Lord of every place and people,

Help me honor the context You have entrusted to me. Teach me to discern season, culture, and capacity wisely. Deliver me from copying what does not belong to me. Let growth emerge organically, rooted in obedience and trust.

Amen.

Chapter 11
From Pastor to Shepherd to Father

"For though ye have ten thousand instructors in Christ, yet have ye not many fathers: for in Christ Jesus I have begotten you through the gospel."

— 1 Corinthians 4:15 (KJV)

Churches often mirror the maturity of their leaders. Not perfectly, and not without grace—but consistently enough to be noticed. When leadership is anxious, congregations feel pressure. When leadership is performative, churches drift toward appearance. When leadership is patient, present, and grounded, churches tend to stabilize, mature, and endure.

This chapter explores a progression that Scripture implies and pastoral experience confirms: leaders often begin as pastors, grow into shepherds, and, over time, are entrusted with the work of spiritual fatherhood. These are not titles to be claimed, but roles that emerge through formation. Each stage carries distinct responsibilities, temptations, and gifts. Understanding the progression helps pastors discern their season and lead without striving to become what they are not yet called to be.

The Pastor: Faithful Laborer of the Word

The term pastor is rooted in the biblical image of feeding. Pastors labor in preaching, teaching, prayer, and care. They are entrusted with the Word and charged to proclaim it faithfully. In many ways, the pastoral role is foundational. It establishes trust, doctrine, and direction.

Scripture emphasizes the seriousness of this calling. James warns that teachers will be judged with greater strictness (James 3:1). Paul exhorts Timothy to "preach the word; be instant in season, out of season" (2 Timothy 4:2 KJV). The pastoral task is demanding and visible. It requires discipline, study, and perseverance.

Early in ministry, pastors often measure fruit by response—attendance, affirmation, and momentum. This is understandable. New leaders seek feedback to discern effectiveness. Yet if leaders remain tethered to immediate response, they risk confusing encouragement with calling. Over time, the pastoral role must deepen beyond performance into presence.

Gordon Fee observes that Paul's letters consistently frame pastoral leadership as service rather than spectacle—labor undertaken for the sake of others' formation.[1] The pastor is not an impresario; he is a steward.

The Shepherd: Presence, Protection, and Care

As pastors mature, many discover that preaching alone does not sustain a congregation. People require care that extends beyond the pulpit. This realization often marks the transition from pastor to shepherd.

Shepherding is relational. It involves knowing people by name, walking with them through suffering, guarding them from harm, and guiding them patiently. Scripture consistently portrays God's leaders as shepherds—Moses, David, the prophets—and Jesus identifies Himself as the Good Shepherd who knows His sheep and lays down His life for them (John 10:11–14).

Peter exhorts elders to "feed the flock of God which is among you" (1 Peter 5:2 KJV). The phrase among you underscores proximity. Shepherds are present. They do not merely instruct; they accompany.

In this stage, leaders often feel the weight of care more acutely. Growth may slow as attention shifts from expansion to health. This is not regression; it is refinement. Churches shepherded well may not grow rapidly, but they often grow deeply.

Henri Nouwen described pastoral leadership as the willingness to enter into people's pain without attempting to control it.[2] Shepherds learn patience. They listen more than they speak. They measure progress not by applause, but by healing.

The Temptation to Skip Shepherding

Modern ministry culture often pressures leaders to bypass shepherding in favor of scaling. Systems are created to manage care. Leaders are encouraged to focus on vision and delegation. While systems can be helpful, bypassing shepherding altogether impoverishes leadership formation.

Leaders who skip shepherding may grow churches numerically while remaining emotionally distant. Over time, trust erodes. Congregations feel managed rather than loved. Growth becomes fragile because it lacks relational glue.

Sociological studies affirm that relational trust is a key predictor of congregational stability.[3] Churches that feel cared for endure change more readily than those that feel directed from afar. Shepherding is not optional; it is formative.

The Father: Generational Leadership

Spiritual fatherhood emerges slowly. It cannot be rushed or self-appointed. It is recognized rather than declared. Paul's words to the Corinthians reveal this distinction clearly: many instructors, few fathers. Instruction transfers information; fatherhood imparts life.

Spiritual fathers invest beyond immediate outcomes. They raise leaders rather than retain control. They celebrate others' success without insecurity. Their concern shifts from my ministry to the next generation. This posture requires deep internal freedom.

Paul exemplifies this role. He refers to Timothy as his "son in the faith" (1 Timothy 1:2). He describes himself as a nursing mother and an encouraging father to the Thessalonian believers (1 Thessalonians 2:7–12). His leadership combined tenderness with authority, patience with conviction.

Walter Brueggemann notes that fatherly leadership in Scripture is generative rather than possessive.[4] Fathers prepare successors. They do not cling to prominence. This posture stands in sharp contrast to leadership driven by legacy anxiety.

Authority That Is Given, Not Grasped

One of the defining marks of spiritual fatherhood is authority that is received rather than seized. Fathers lead from trust, not from position. Their authority rests on proven faithfulness, not on charisma.

Jesus distinguished between worldly authority and kingdom authority. "The princes of the Gentiles exercise dominion," He said, "but it shall not be so among you" (Matthew 20:25–26 KJV). Kingdom leadership is marked by service.

Spiritual fathers embody this paradox. They possess influence without coercion. Their words carry weight because their lives have carried responsibility. Younger leaders seek them out not because they demand allegiance, but because they offer wisdom.

Research on leadership longevity consistently affirms that leaders who mentor others and share authority experience greater sustainability and impact.[5] Fatherhood multiplies leadership rather than consolidating it.

How Leadership Maturity Shapes Growth

Church growth is profoundly affected by leadership maturity. Pastors focused primarily on preaching may grow congregations through clarity and vision. Shepherds stabilize churches through care and trust. Fathers extend impact beyond a single congregation by raising leaders and networks.

None of these expressions is superior in isolation. They are sequential and complementary. Problems arise when leaders remain fixed in one mode beyond its season.

- Pastors who never shepherd may produce crowds without care.
- Shepherds who never release may create healthy but insular communities.
- Fathers who disengage prematurely may abandon present responsibilities.

Discernment lies in knowing one's season.

The Burden Lifted by Maturity

As leaders mature into fatherhood, the burden of growth often lifts. Fathers are less anxious about numbers because their confidence rests in reproduction, not accumulation. They measure success by whom they have raised, not by what they have built.

This shift brings freedom. Churches sense it. Leadership becomes calm rather than urgent. Vision becomes spacious rather than pressured. Growth, when it comes, is received rather than driven.

Eugene Peterson observed that pastoral maturity is marked by "a long obedience in the same direction."[6] Fathers embody this obedience. They endure.

The Role of Oversight and Networks

Spiritual fatherhood often extends beyond a single congregation into networks of leaders and churches. The New Testament reflects this pattern through apostolic oversight. Paul maintained relationships with multiple congregations, offering counsel, correction, and encouragement.

Such oversight was relational, not bureaucratic. Authority flowed through relationship and shared mission. This model offers a corrective to both isolation and control. Leaders were neither alone nor micromanaged.

Modern church networks function healthiest when they reflect this fathering posture—supportive rather than coercive, formative rather than performative.

Discerning Your Current Season

Not every leader is called to function as a father in the same way or at the same time. Seasons differ. Some pastors are called to long-term shepherding within a single congregation. Others are entrusted with broader oversight later in life.

Discernment requires honesty. Leaders must resist the temptation to adopt roles prematurely. Fatherhood without formation becomes authoritarian. Shepherding without depth becomes enabling. Pastoring without growth becomes stagnant.

The Spirit guides leaders into appropriate seasons when they are ready to receive them.

Preparing the Next Generation

Spiritual fathers prioritize succession. They do not assume their indispensability. They prepare others to lead faithfully beyond them. This preparation is one of the clearest indicators of maturity.

Paul instructed Timothy to entrust what he had learned to faithful people who could teach others also (2 Timothy 2:2). This generational vision ensures continuity without dependence on a single personality.

Churches led by fathers tend to endure transitions more peacefully. Growth becomes sustainable because leadership is shared.

Freedom Through Fatherhood

This chapter invites pastors to embrace maturity without anxiety. Growth is no longer something to prove; it is something to steward. Leadership becomes less about visibility and more about vitality.

When pastors mature into shepherds and shepherds into fathers, churches often experience a deeper, steadier form of growth—one rooted in trust, care, and generational impact.

The next chapter will explore when faithfulness leads to increase—how God often honors obedience with growth, and how pastors can receive increase without returning to pressure or performance.

Early Episcopal Fatherhood

In the early church, **bishops were spiritual fathers, not CEOs**. Figures like Cyprian of Carthage and Athanasius guided churches through persecution and doctrinal crisis with paternal authority rooted in relationship and sacrifice.

Reflection Prayer

Father of all generations,

Mature my leadership according to Your timing. Teach me to shepherd patiently and to father generously. Free me from insecurity so I can raise others faithfully. Let my leadership reproduce life, not dependency.

Amen.

Chapter 12

When Faithfulness Leads to Increase

> "Well done, thou good and faithful servant… thou hast been faithful over a few things, I will make thee ruler over many things."
>
> — Matthew 25:21 (KJV)

One of the quiet fears many pastors carry is that emphasizing faithfulness over growth may sound like resignation. It can feel as though celebrating obedience without visible increase is merely a way of coping with disappointment. Scripture, however, tells a different story. Faithfulness is not God's consolation prize; it is His chosen pathway. And often—though not always—increase follows faithfulness.

This chapter explores how Scripture frames increase, why it must never be demanded, and how pastors can receive growth without returning to the burdens of performance and comparison.

Increase Is God's Initiative

From Genesis onward, increase is portrayed as God's work. The first command to humanity—"be fruitful, and multiply" (Genesis 1:28)—establishes fruitfulness as a divine blessing, not a human achievement. Throughout Scripture, increase is consistently attributed to God's initiative.

Paul states this explicitly: "I have planted, Apollos watered; but God gave the increase" (1 Corinthians 3:6 KJV). The grammar is instructive. Human responsibility ends with faithfulness in assigned tasks. Increase remains God's prerogative.

When pastors attempt to control increase, they cross a theological boundary. They assume responsibility Scripture reserves for God. This assumption is the root of much pastoral burden.

Gordon Fee notes that Paul's insistence on God as the source of growth was corrective, aimed at dismantling competitive leadership cultures already present in the early church.[1] The same correction is needed today.

Biblical Patterns of Increase After Faithfulness

Scripture offers numerous examples where increase followed long seasons of obedience rather than strategic pursuit.

- Abraham waited decades before seeing the fulfillment of God's promise. His faithfulness was tested through delay, uncertainty, and sacrifice. Increase came in God's time, not Abraham's.
- Joseph remained faithful through betrayal, imprisonment, and obscurity before being elevated. His increase was not the product of ambition, but of integrity.
- David was anointed king long before he ascended the throne. Faithfulness in obscurity preceded authority in visibility.
- The early church devoted itself to prayer, teaching, fellowship, and care—and then "the Lord added to the church daily" (Acts 2:47).

These patterns reveal a consistent truth: increase is often delayed until character, capacity, and calling align.

Walter Brueggemann observes that biblical faith resists immediacy. God's promises unfold through patience rather than acceleration.[2] Increase divorced from preparation becomes destructive rather than sustaining.

Faithfulness Does Not Guarantee Increase

It is important to state clearly what Scripture does not promise. Faithfulness does not guarantee numerical growth, public recognition, or expanded influence. Many faithful servants never experienced visible increase in their lifetime.

Jeremiah preached faithfully for decades with little response. Ezekiel ministered among resistant hearers. John the Baptist's ministry decreased by design. Jesus Himself was rejected and crucified.

Faithfulness is not a formula for success; it is a posture of obedience. Increase may come—or it may not. Yet faithfulness remains fully pleasing to God.

This truth protects pastors from transactional theology—the belief that obedience obligates God to reward in specific ways. Such thinking reduces God to a mechanism and faith to leverage.

Dietrich Bonhoeffer warned against equating faithfulness with outcomes, noting that obedience is validated by relationship with Christ, not by visible success.[3]

When Increase Does Come

When increase does come, Scripture frames it as entrustment, not entitlement. Jesus' parable of the talents makes this distinction clear. The servants who were faithful over little were entrusted with more—not because they demanded it, but because they proved trustworthy.

Increase tests leaders as much as it blesses them. Visibility amplifies weaknesses. Expansion exposes gaps. Responsibility multiplies pressure.

Many pastors are unprepared for this test because they have been taught to pursue growth rather than steward it. When increase arrives, they revert to performance-driven patterns— overworking, overpromising, and overextending.

Scripture calls leaders to receive increase with humility. Paul repeatedly deflected credit for his ministry's fruit, emphasizing grace rather than ability (1 Corinthians 15:10). Increase did not inflate his ego; it deepened his dependence.

Capacity Must Grow With Influence

One of the dangers of increase is assuming that faithfulness alone is sufficient to sustain it. Scripture suggests otherwise. When God entrusts more, leaders must grow accordingly.

Moses' leadership nearly collapsed under the weight of increased responsibility until Jethro advised delegation and shared leadership (Exodus 18). The apostles faced similar strain in Acts 6 and responded by expanding leadership structures.

Increase requires:
- Expanded leadership
- Clear delegation
- Strengthened accountability
- Sustained spiritual disciplines

Without these, growth becomes unsustainable.

Peter Drucker observed that success often creates complexity faster than leaders anticipate.[4] Churches are not exempt. Increase demands wisdom as well as faith.

Receiving Increase Without Losing the Soul

Perhaps the greatest danger of increase is losing the very practices that made faithfulness possible. Prayer is crowded out by meetings. Presence is replaced by performance. Shepherding gives way to management.

Jesus modeled a different way. Even as His influence grew, He withdrew to pray. He guarded solitude. He remained anchored to the Father.

Eugene Peterson warned that pastors who do not protect their inner life will inevitably substitute busyness for faithfulness.[5] Increase that costs intimacy with God is too expensive.

Pastors must learn to receive growth without allowing it to redefine success. Faithfulness remains the measure, regardless of scale.

Increase as Shared Joy

Scripture consistently portrays increase as communal rather than individual. Growth belongs to the body, not the leader. Paul celebrated the fruit of others' labor. He rejoiced in churches he did not personally lead.

When pastors internalize growth as personal validation, they carry unnecessary pressure. When they release it as shared stewardship, joy replaces anxiety.

James Dunn notes that early Christian leaders understood growth as participation in God's mission rather than proof of individual effectiveness.[6] This perspective guards humility and fosters collaboration.

The Danger of Chasing Past Blessings

Another subtle danger arises after increase has occurred. Pastors may attempt to preserve or replicate a season of growth rather than remaining attentive to God's present leading. Yesterday's blessing becomes today's burden.

Scripture warns against this fixation. Israel often longed for past deliverances rather than trusting God in the present. Jesus cautioned against storing old wine in new skins.

Faithfulness requires attentiveness to what God is doing now, not nostalgia for what He did then.

Redefining Success After Increase

Perhaps the most important work pastors must do after increase is redefine success again. Growth has a way of reintroducing false metrics. Attendance rises. Influence expands. Expectations multiply.

Leaders must return repeatedly to Christ's definition: obedience, love, endurance, truth, humility. These measures remain constant regardless of size.

Revelation's letters were written to churches at varying stages of development. Christ's criteria did not change. Faithfulness remained the standard.

Increase That Does Not Burden

When increase is received as gift rather than goal, it blesses rather than burdens. Leaders steward it prayerfully. Churches grow steadily. Anxiety diminishes.

Pastors who understand this paradox experience freedom. They work diligently without striving. They plan wisely without panic. They rejoice in fruit without clinging to it.

Increase becomes testimony, not trophy.

Trusting God With Outcomes

This chapter calls pastors to trust God with outcomes. Faithfulness remains their responsibility. Increase remains God's prerogative.

When pastors release control, ministry becomes lighter. Growth loses its power to define worth. Faithfulness regains its central place.

The next chapter will move toward the Conclusion and Final Charge, drawing together the book's themes and offering a pastoral invitation to lead free from false measures of success.

Delayed Recognition of Faithful Leaders

Many of history's most influential Christian leaders—Patrick of Ireland, William Carey, Hudson Taylor—saw limited results initially. Their long-term influence became clear only **after years of patient obedience,** reinforcing that increase often follows faithfulness slowly.

Reflection Prayer

Giver of increase,

Help me receive growth as stewardship, not validation. Guard my heart when influence expands. Teach me to remain faithful in abundance as in scarcity. Let increase deepen my dependence, not diminish my devotion.

Amen.

Chapter 13

A Word to the Discouraged Pastor

"And let us not be weary in well doing: for in due season we
shall reap, if we faint not."

— Galatians 6:9 (KJV)

There is a kind of discouragement that does not come from
failure, but from faithfulness without visible fruit. It settles in
quietly, often after years of consistent labor. Sermons have been
preached. Prayers have been prayed. People have been loved,
buried, counseled, married, restored, and sometimes lost. Yet
the numbers remain stubbornly the same. The room does not
fill. The recognition does not come. The breakthrough does not
arrive.

And the pastor begins to wonder—How long can I keep going
like this?

This chapter is written to that pastor.

Not the one who quit praying.
Not the one who compromised doctrine.
Not the one who abandoned the call.
But the one who kept showing up—and is tired.

Discouragement Is Not Disobedience

Scripture never equates discouragement with unfaithfulness.
Some of the most faithful servants of God experienced profound
discouragement precisely because they were obedient.

Jeremiah was faithful—and deeply discouraged. He lamented his calling, cursed the day of his birth, and questioned whether his obedience had cost him everything (Jeremiah 20:7–18). Elijah was faithful—and exhausted. After a public victory, he collapsed under the weight of fear and isolation (1 Kings 19:1–4). Even Paul spoke openly of being "pressed out of measure, above strength" (2 Corinthians 1:8).

Discouragement is not evidence that something is wrong with your faith.

It is often evidence that you have been faithful for a long time without relief.

Walter Brueggemann notes that biblical faith makes room for lament precisely because obedience does not always produce immediate consolation.[1] Faithfulness and weariness often coexist.

Slow Growth Is Still Growth

One of the cruel lies discouragement whispers is that nothing is happening. Scripture contradicts this assumption repeatedly. Growth in God's economy is often imperceptible before it is undeniable.

Jesus likened the kingdom to seed scattered into soil—growing *"he knoweth not how"* (Mark 4:27). The farmer does not control the process. He trusts it. Growth happens underground long before it appears above ground.

Pastoral discouragement often stems from confusing visibility with vitality. You may not see growth, but formation may be happening quietly:

- A believer learning to forgive
- A marriage choosing endurance

- A young leader maturing slowly
- A congregation learning to pray

These are not small things. They are eternal things.

James reminds believers that patience produces maturity (James 1:4). Maturity rarely announces itself loudly.

The Loneliness of Unseen Faithfulness

Few people understand how lonely faithful ministry can be. Applause is rare. Feedback is minimal. Criticism travels faster than encouragement. And pastors are often expected to remain strong without admitting weakness.

Paul's words to Timothy reveal this loneliness: "Only Luke is with me" (2 Timothy 4:11). Even apostolic leaders experienced seasons of abandonment. Faithfulness does not immunize leaders from isolation.

Eugene Peterson described pastoral ministry as a vocation largely lived "without applause," requiring leaders to learn contentment with obscurity.[2] This obscurity is not punishment; it is often protection—guarding the pastor from confusing approval with calling.

Guarding the Heart from Comparison

Comparison is one of discouragement's most effective weapons. It rarely attacks doctrine; it attacks identity. Why is their church growing and mine isn't? What am I missing? What did I do wrong?

Scripture speaks directly to this temptation. Paul warns against measuring ourselves by one another, calling it unwise (2 Corinthians 10:12). Comparison distorts perspective because it ignores context, calling, and assignment.

Peter fell into this trap when he asked Jesus about John's future. Jesus' response was firm and freeing: "What is that to thee? follow thou me" (John 21:22).

Comparison distracts from obedience. It turns faithfulness into competition. It burdens pastors with expectations God never assigned.

Guarding the heart means actively resisting narratives that tie worth to outcomes. It means returning repeatedly to Christ's call: Follow Me.

Obedience Without Applause

One of the hardest lessons in ministry is learning to obey without affirmation. Applause can be intoxicating; its absence can be crushing. Yet Scripture consistently affirms obedience that is unseen by people and fully seen by God.

Jesus taught that faithfulness practiced in secret is rewarded by the Father who sees in secret (Matthew 6:1–6). Much of pastoral ministry lives in this hidden place—where prayers are whispered, tears are shed privately, and obedience goes unnoticed.

Hebrews speaks of faithful saints who "obtained a good report through faith" yet never saw the fulfillment of promises in their lifetime (Hebrews 11:39). Their obedience mattered, even without visible reward.

Dietrich Bonhoeffer reminds us that obedience is validated by Christ's call, not by public success.[3] Faithfulness is not less faithful because it is unseen.

Endurance Is a Spiritual Discipline

Endurance is not passive resignation; it is active trust. Scripture treats endurance as a fruit of faith, forged through perseverance rather than comfort.

Paul describes endurance as something God works into believers through suffering (Romans 5:3–4). James links endurance to spiritual completeness. Revelation praises churches not for growth, but for perseverance.

Pastoral endurance is cultivated, not accidental. It is sustained through:

- Prayer that is honest, not performative
- Scripture that anchors identity
- Relationships that allow vulnerability
- Rhythms that protect the soul

Endurance does not mean ignoring exhaustion. It means tending to the soul so obedience remains possible.

When Obedience Feels Like Failure

One of the most painful distortions discouragement creates is the feeling that obedience itself has failed. If I were truly faithful, wouldn't this look different by now?

Scripture dismantles this lie. Noah preached righteousness for decades with no visible response. Jeremiah ministered faithfully without national repentance. John the Baptist decreased intentionally. Jesus Himself was crucified.

If obedience were measured by immediate results, Scripture's heroes would be failures.

Karl Barth warned against interpreting faithfulness through the lens of outcome rather than calling.[4] Obedience stands on God's command, not on its reception.

The God Who Sees the Unseen

The deepest comfort for the discouraged pastor is this: God sees what others never will.

He sees the sermons preached when attendance was low.
He sees the prayers prayed when no one responded.
He sees the faithfulness that never made headlines.

Hebrews assures believers that God is not unjust to forget their work and labor of love (Hebrews 6:10). Faithfulness is never wasted. It is recorded in heaven even when ignored on earth.

Revelation's repeated phrase—"I know thy works"—is not a threat. It is a promise. Christ sees.

Keeping Going When Growth Feels Slow

So how do you keep going?
Not by pretending it doesn't hurt.
Not by chasing someone else's outcome.
Not by redefining faithfulness to fit culture.

You keep going by returning—again and again—to the simplicity of your call.

You were called to preach the Word.
You were called to shepherd people.
You were called to obey Christ.

Everything else is secondary.

Pastors who endure are not those who never feel discouraged, but those who refuse to let discouragement redefine obedience.

A Father's Word to the Weary

If you are tired, that does not disqualify you.

If you are discouraged, that does not mean you have failed.

If growth feels slow, that does not mean God is absent.

Faithfulness is still faithfulness—even when it is quiet.

And one day, beyond metrics and milestones, beyond applause and affirmation, there is a word that outweighs every earthly measure:

"Well done."

Not *well known*. Not *well attended*. But *well done*.

Keep going.

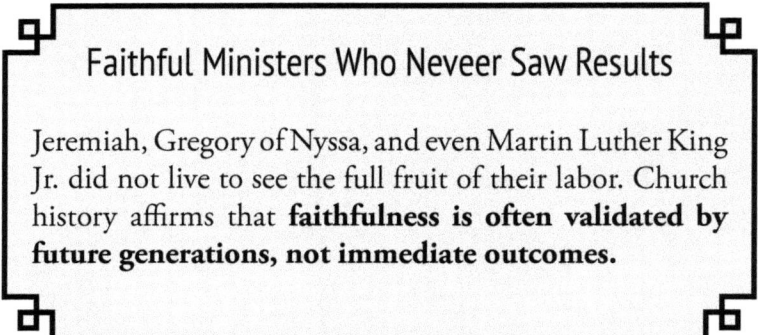

Faithful Ministers Who Neveer Saw Results

Jeremiah, Gregory of Nyssa, and even Martin Luther King Jr. did not live to see the full fruit of their labor. Church history affirms that **faithfulness is often validated by future generations, not immediate outcomes.**

Reflection Prayer

God who sees the unseen,

You know my weariness and You honor my obedience. Strengthen me where discouragement has settled. Guard my heart from comparison and despair. Help me keep going—not in my strength, but in Yours.

Amen.

Conclusion
Well Done Is Greater Than Well Known

"Moreover it is required in stewards, that a man be found faithful."

— 1 Corinthians 4:2 (KJV)

Every pastor reaches a moment—sometimes quietly, sometimes painfully—when the question of success demands an answer. Not the question asked by conferences, denominations, or peers, but the one whispered in prayer, late at night, when the work is heavy and the room feels small:

Has my faithfulness mattered?

This book was written to answer that question—not with sentiment, but with Scripture; not with platitudes, but with perspective. And the answer Scripture gives is consistent, clear, and freeing:

God is not impressed by what we build.

He is pleased by how we obey.

The burden many pastors carry was never meant to be theirs. It did not come from Christ. It came from borrowed measures, cultural expectations, and unspoken comparisons that slowly replaced obedience with outcomes. This conclusion is an invitation to lay that burden down—for good.

Success According to Heaven

The most sobering reality for any leader is this: every ministry will eventually be evaluated—but not by the metrics we are tempted to use.

Jesus' final assessment of His servants does not begin with numbers, reach, or reputation. It begins with stewardship. "Well done, thou good and faithful servant." The commendation is not for scale, but for faithfulness. Not for expansion, but for obedience.

Paul understood this clearly. Writing to the Corinthians—a church enamored with visibility and personality—he reminded them that leadership is stewardship, and the only requirement is faithfulness (1 Corinthians 4:2). This single verse dismantles an entire culture of performance-based ministry.

Walter Brueggemann observes that biblical faith consistently resists defining success by public achievement, insisting instead on covenant loyalty and trust in God's unseen work.[1] Heaven's economy does not reward visibility; it honors obedience.

The Illusion of Being Well Known

In every generation, there is pressure to be seen. Platforms promise impact. Visibility masquerades as influence. Being well known is often mistaken for being effective.

Scripture offers no such equation.

Jesus Himself was rejected by many, misunderstood by crowds, and abandoned by followers. Yet no life has ever been more faithful, more fruitful, or more significant. The cross—an apparent failure by worldly standards—became the means of redemption for the world.

The early church did not pursue recognition; it pursued faithfulness. Its leaders were often obscure, persecuted, and unseen. Yet their obedience reshaped history.

Eugene Peterson warned that pastors who confuse recognition with faithfulness eventually exchange vocation for career.[2] Being well known may feel validating, but it cannot sustain the soul. Only obedience can do that.

The Quiet Power of Being Well Done

There is a power in quiet faithfulness that is rarely celebrated and never forgotten by God. Scripture assures us that God sees what is done in secret. He records what others overlook. He remembers what seems wasted.

Hebrews declares that God is not unjust to forget the labor of love shown in faithful service (Hebrews 6:10). Revelation's repeated assurance—"I know thy works"—is not a threat, but a comfort. Christ sees.

Pastors who labor faithfully in small places, obscure settings, or slow seasons are not invisible. They are seen by the only One whose evaluation endures.

Dietrich Bonhoeffer insisted that obedience gains its meaning not from success, but from relationship with Christ.[3] Faithfulness does not require witnesses to be valid.

Letting Go of False Measures

To finish well, pastors must release measures that God never assigned:

- The pressure to outgrow others
- The need to justify one's calling through numbers
- The anxiety of comparison
- The fear of being forgotten

These measures are heavy because they were never meant to be carried.

Jesus' invitation remains the same: "Take my yoke upon you… for my yoke is easy, and my burden is light" (Matthew 11:29–30). When ministry feels crushing, it is often because we have taken on a yoke that is not His.

Letting go is an act of faith.

Faithfulness Across a Lifetime

Scripture does not celebrate leaders who burn brightly and briefly, but those who endure. Paul's final testimony was not about how many he reached, but how faithfully he finished: "I have fought a good fight, I have finished my course, I have kept the faith" (2 Timothy 4:7).

Endurance is not accidental. It is cultivated through humility, obedience, repentance, and trust. Pastors who finish well are those who consistently return to the simplicity of their call, even when ministry becomes complex.

James Dunn notes that early Christian leaders understood their work as participation in God's mission rather than personal achievement.[4] This posture guarded them against despair and pride alike.

A Final Word to Pastors

If you are still preaching the Word—keep going.
If you are still loving people—keep going.
If you are still praying when it feels unseen—keep going.

You are not behind.
You are not forgotten.
You are not failing because your faithfulness looks ordinary.

Ordinary obedience is the soil where God does His deepest work.

A Pastoral Charge

So here is the charge with which this book concludes:

Do not measure your ministry by what impresses people.
Measure it by what pleases Christ.

Do not envy assignments you were never given.
Steward the one entrusted to you.

Do not despise slow seasons.
They are often where roots grow deepest.

Do not exchange obedience for applause.
Applause fades. Obedience endures.

And when your work is done—whether known by many or few—may you stand before Christ unburdened by comparison, free from false measures, and confident in this alone:

Well done is greater than well known.

The Forgotten Faithful

History remembers many pastors and leaders whose names never became famous, yet whose faithfulness sustained communities, preserved Scripture, and raised generations of believers. Heaven's record book is far more complete than ours.

Reflection Prayer

Faithful Lord,

I release every false measure of success. I choose obedience over recognition, faithfulness over fame. Teach me to finish well, trusting You with outcomes. May my life and ministry echo this one desire: *Well done.*

Amen.

Endnotes

Introduction

1. Mark Chaves et al., *Congregations in America* (Cambridge, MA: Harvard University Press, 2004), 17–22; Pew Research Center, "America's Changing Religious Landscape," 2015.
2. Gordon D. Fee, *The First Epistle to the Corinthians, New International Commentary on the New Testament* (Grand Rapids: Eerdmans, 1987), 173–176.
3. Dietrich Bonhoeffer, *The Cost of Discipleship* (New York: Macmillan, 1963), 43–47.
4. Craig R. Koester, *Revelation: A New Translation with Introduction and Commentary, Anchor Yale Bible* (New Haven: Yale University Press, 2014), 229–241.
5. Eugene H. Peterson, *A Long Obedience in the Same Direction* (Downers Grove, IL: InterVarsity Press, 1980), 15–18.
6. Nancy T. Ammerman, *Congregation and Community* (New Brunswick, NJ: Rutgers University Press, 1997), 43–58.
7. Alan Kreider, *The Patient Ferment of the Early Church* (Grand Rapids: Baker Academic, 2016), 55–82.

Chapter 1

1. Gordon D. Fee, *The First Epistle to the Corinthians, New International Commentary on the New Testament* (Grand Rapids: Eerdmans, 1987), 131–136.
2. Mark Chaves, *Congregations in America* (Cambridge, MA: Harvard University Press, 2004), 17–22.
3. Dietrich Bonhoeffer, *The Cost of Discipleship* (New York: Macmillan, 1963), 43–47.

4. Craig R. Koester, *Revelation: A New Translation with Introduction and Commentary, Anchor Yale Bible* (New Haven: Yale University Press, 2014), 229–241.
5. Alan Kreider, *The Patient Ferment of the Early Church* (Grand Rapids: Baker Academic, 2016), 55–82.
6. Eugene H. Peterson, *A Long Obedience in the Same Direction* (Downers Grove, IL: InterVarsity Press, 1980), 15–18.

Chapter 2

1. Mark Chaves, *Congregations in America* (Cambridge, MA: Harvard University Press, 2004), 17–25.
2. H. B. London Jr. and Neil B. Wiseman, *Pastors at Greater Risk* (Ventura, CA: Regal Books, 2003), 31–46.

Chapter 3

1. Craig R. Koester, *Revelation: A New Translation with Introduction and Commentary, Anchor Yale Bible* (New Haven: Yale University Press, 2014), 229–245.
2. Dietrich Bonhoeffer, *The Cost of Discipleship* (New York: Macmillan, 1963), 43–47.

Chapter 4

1. Mark Chaves, *Congregations in America* (Cambridge, MA: Harvard University Press, 2004), 17–25.
2. Walter Brueggemann, *The Prophetic Imagination,* 2nd ed. (Minneapolis: Fortress Press, 2001), 24–31.
3. Wayne A. Meeks, *The First Urban Christians* (New Haven: Yale University Press, 1983), 75–98.
4. Alan Kreider, *The Patient Ferment of the Early Church* (Grand Rapids: Baker Academic, 2016), 55–82.

5. Gordon D. Fee, *God's Empowering Presence* (Peabody, MA: Hendrickson, 1994), 689–702.
6. Nancy T. Ammerman, *Congregation and Community* (New Brunswick, NJ: Rutgers University Press, 1997), 43–58.
7. H. B. London Jr. and Neil B. Wiseman, *Pastors at Greater Risk* (Ventura, CA: Regal Books, 2003), 31–46.

Chapter 5

1. Richard Bauckham, *Bible and Mission* (Grand Rapids: Baker Academic, 2003), 78–92.
2. Wayne A. Meeks, *The First Urban Christians* (New Haven: Yale University Press, 1983), 75–103.
3. Alan Kreider, *The Patient Ferment of the Early Church* (Grand Rapids: Baker Academic, 2016), 55–82.
4. Rodney Stark, *The Rise of Christianity* (Princeton, NJ: Princeton University Press, 1996), 3–29.
5. Tertullian, *Apologeticus,* chap. 50.
6. John Howard Yoder, T*he Politics of Jesus,* 2nd ed. (Grand Rapids: Eerdmans, 1994), 146–162.
7. Nancy T. Ammerman, *Congregation and Community* (New Brunswick, NJ: Rutgers University Press, 1997), 43–58.

Chapter 6

1. Darrell L. Bock, *Jesus According to Scripture* (Grand Rapids: Baker Academic, 2002), 269–276.
2. Dallas Willard, *The Great Omission* (San Francisco: HarperOne, 2006), 4–11.
3. N. T. Wright, *Jesus and the Victory of God* (Minneapolis: Fortress Press, 1996), 182–190.
4. Walter Brueggemann, *The Prophetic Imagination,* 2nd ed. (Minneapolis: Fortress Press, 2001), 38–45.

5. Alan Kreider, *The Patient Ferment of the Early Church* (Grand Rapids: Baker Academic, 2016), 83–110.
6. Christian A. Schwarz, *Natural Church Development* (St. Charles, IL: ChurchSmart Resources, 1996), 33–48.
7. Dietrich Bonhoeffer, *The Cost of Discipleship* (New York: Macmillan, 1963), 43–47.
8. James D. G. Dunn, *The Acts of the Apostles* (Valley Forge, PA: Trinity Press International, 1996), 63–70.

Chapter 7

1. Dallas Willard, *The Spirit of the Disciplines* (San Francisco: Harper & Row, 1988), 153–170.
2. Nancy T. Ammerman, *Congregation and Community* (New Brunswick, NJ: Rutgers University Press, 1997), 43–58.
3. Robert J. Clinton, *The Making of a Leader* (Colorado Springs: NavPress, 1988), 101–122.
4. Rodney Stark, *The Rise of Christianity* (Princeton, NJ: Princeton University Press, 1996), 3–29.
5. Gordon D. Fee, *God's Empowering Presence* (Peabody, MA: Hendrickson, 1994), 689–702.
6. Christian A. Schwarz, *Natural Church Development* (St. Charles, IL: ChurchSmart Resources, 1996), 33–48.
7. Walter Brueggemann, *The Prophetic Imagination,* 2nd ed. (Minneapolis: Fortress Press, 2001), 67–75.

Chapter 8

1. Robert J. Clinton, *The Making of a Leader* (Colorado Springs: NavPress, 1988), 101–122.
2. Dallas Willard, *The Great Omission* (San Francisco: HarperOne, 2006), 4–11.

3. Dietrich Bonhoeffer, *The Cost of Discipleship* (New York: Macmillan, 1963), 43–47.

4. H. B. London Jr. and Neil B. Wiseman, *Pastors at Greater Risk* (Ventura, CA: Regal Books, 2003), 31–46.

5. Eugene H. Peterson, *Working the Angles* (Grand Rapids: Eerdmans, 1987), 1–18.

6. Nancy T. Ammerman, *Congregation and Community* (New Brunswick, NJ: Rutgers University Press, 1997), 59–74.

Chapter 9

1. Andy Crouch, *Strong and Weak* (Downers Grove, IL: InterVarsity Press, 2016), 89–104.

2. Karl Barth, *Homiletics* (Louisville: Westminster John Knox Press, 1991), 89–94.

3. Christian A. Schwarz, *Natural Church Development* (St. Charles, IL: ChurchSmart Resources, 1996), 33–48.

4. Eugene H. Peterson, *Working the Angles* (Grand Rapids: Eerdmans, 1987), 1–18.

5. Nancy T. Ammerman, *Congregation and Community* (New Brunswick, NJ: Rutgers University Press, 1997), 59–74.

6. James K. A. Smith, *You Are What You Love* (Grand Rapids: Brazos Press, 2016), 25–44.

7. Patrick Lencioni, *The Five Dysfunctions of a Team* (San Francisco: Jossey-Bass, 2002), 195–214.

8. Walter Brueggemann, *The Prophetic Imagination,* 2nd ed. (Minneapolis: Fortress Press, 2001), 38–45.

Chapter 10

1. Andrew F. Walls, *The Missionary Movement in Christian History* (Maryknoll, NY: Orbis Books, 1996), 26–42.

2. Gordon D. Fee, *Paul, the Spirit, and the People of God* (Peabody, MA: Hendrickson, 1996), 45–61.
3. Nancy T. Ammerman, *Congregation and Community* (New Brunswick, NJ: Rutgers University Press, 1997), 75–92.
4. Peter Drucker, *Managing the Non-Profit Organization* (New York: HarperCollins, 1990), 23–39.
5. Lesslie Newbigin, *The Gospel in a Pluralist Society* (Grand Rapids: Eerdmans, 1989), 141–158.
6. Walter Brueggemann, *The Prophetic Imagination,* 2nd ed. (Minneapolis: Fortress Press, 2001), 67–75.

Chapter 11

1. Gordon D. Fee, *Paul, the Spirit, and the People of God* (Peabody, MA: Hendrickson, 1996), 63–78.
2. Henri J. M. Nouwen, *The Wounded Healer* (New York: Image Books, 1979), 88–95.
3. Nancy T. Ammerman, *Congregation and Community* (New Brunswick, NJ: Rutgers University Press, 1997), 93–109.
4. Walter Brueggemann, *The Prophetic Imagination,* 2nd ed. (Minneapolis: Fortress Press, 2001), 67–75.
5. Robert J. Clinton, *The Making of a Leader* (Colorado Springs: NavPress, 1988), 189–206.
6. Eugene H. Peterson, *A Long Obedience in the Same Direction* (Downers Grove, IL: InterVarsity Press, 1980), 15–18.

Chapter 12

1. Gordon D. Fee, *The First Epistle to the Corinthians, NICNT* (Grand Rapids: Eerdmans, 1987), 132–136.
2. Walter Brueggemann, *The Prophetic Imagination,* 2nd ed. (Minneapolis: Fortress Press, 2001), 38–45.

3. Dietrich Bonhoeffer, *The Cost of Discipleship* (New York: Macmillan, 1963), 43–47.
4. Peter F. Drucker, *Managing the Non-Profit Organization* (New York: HarperCollins, 1990), 47–58.
5. Eugene H. Peterson, *Working the Angles* (Grand Rapids: Eerdmans, 1987), 1–18.
6. James D. G. Dunn, *The Acts of the Apostles* (Valley Forge, PA: Trinity Press International, 1996), 63–70.

Chapter 13

1. Walter Brueggemann, *The Message of the Psalms* (Minneapolis: Augsburg Publishing House, 1984), 51–58.
2. Eugene H. Peterson, *The Contemplative Pastor* (Grand Rapids: Eerdmans, 1989), 22–34.
3. Dietrich Bonhoeffer, *The Cost of Discipleship* (New York: Macmillan, 1963), 63–69.
4. Karl Barth, *Church Dogmatics,* vol. IV/3 (Edinburgh: T&T Clark, 1961), 872–880.

Conclusion

1. Walter Brueggemann, *The Prophetic Imagination,* 2nd ed. (Minneapolis: Fortress Press, 2001), 38–45.
2. Eugene H. Peterson, *The Contemplative Pastor* (Grand Rapids: Eerdmans, 1989), 15–29.
3. Dietrich Bonhoeffer, *The Cost of Discipleship* (New York: Macmillan, 1963), 63–69.
4. James D. G. Dunn, *The Acts of the Apostles* (Valley Forge, PA: Trinity Press International, 1996), 305–312.

Bibliography

Ammerman, Nancy T. *Congregation and Community.* New Brunswick, NJ: Rutgers University Press, 1997.

Barth, Karl. *Church Dogmatics.* Vol. IV/3. Edinburgh: T&T Clark, 1961.

———. *Homiletics.* Louisville: Westminster John Knox Press, 1991.

Bauckham, Richard. *Bible and Mission: Christian Witness in a Postmodern World.* Grand Rapids: Baker Academic, 2003.

Bock, Darrell L. *Jesus According to Scripture: Restoring the Portrait from the Gospels.* Grand Rapids: Baker Academic, 2002.

Bonhoeffer, Dietrich. *The Cost of Discipleship.* New York: Macmillan, 1963.

Brueggemann, Walter. *The Message of the Psalms: A Theological Commentary.* Minneapolis: Augsburg Publishing House, 1984.

———. *The Prophetic Imagination.* 2nd ed. Minneapolis: Fortress Press, 2001.

Chaves, Mark. *Congregations in America.* Cambridge, MA: Harvard University Press, 2004.

Clinton, Robert J. *The Making of a Leader.* Colorado Springs: NavPress, 1988.

Crouch, Andy. *Strong and Weak: Embracing a Life of Love, Risk, and True Flourishing.* Downers Grove, IL: InterVarsity Press, 2016.

Drucker, Peter F. *Managing the Non-Profit Organization: Principles and Practices*. New York: HarperCollins, 1990.

Dunn, James D. G. *The Acts of the Apostles*. Valley Forge, PA: Trinity Press International, 1996.

Fee, Gordon D. *God's Empowering Presence: The Holy Spirit in the Letters of Paul*. Peabody, MA: Hendrickson, 1994.

———. *Paul, the Spirit, and the People of God*. Peabody, MA: Hendrickson, 1996.

———. *The First Epistle to the Corinthians*. New International Commentary on the New Testament. Grand Rapids: Eerdmans, 1987.

Kreider, Alan. *The Patient Ferment of the Early Church: The Improbable Rise of Christianity in the Roman Empire*. Grand Rapids: Baker Academic, 2016.

Koester, Craig R. *Revelation: A New Translation with Introduction and Commentary. Anchor Yale Bible*. New Haven: Yale University Press, 2014.

London Jr., H. B., and Neil B. Wiseman. *Pastors at Greater Risk*. Ventura, CA: Regal Books, 2003.

Meeks, Wayne A. T*he First Urban Christians: The Social World of the Apostle Paul*. New Haven: Yale University Press, 1983.

Newbigin, Lesslie. *The Gospel in a Pluralist Society*. Grand Rapids: Eerdmans, 1989.

Nouwen, Henri J. M. *The Wounded Healer: Ministry in Contemporary Society*. New York: Image Books, 1979.

Peterson, Eugene H. *A Long Obedience in the Same Direction: Discipleship in an Instant Society.* Downers Grove, IL: InterVarsity Press, 1980.

———. *The Contemplative Pastor: Returning to the Art of Spiritual Direction.* Grand Rapids: Eerdmans, 1989.

———. *Working the Angles: The Shape of Pastoral Integrity.* Grand Rapids: Eerdmans, 1987.

Schwarz, Christian A. *Natural Church Development: A Guide to Eight Essential Qualities of Healthy Churches.* St. Charles, IL: ChurchSmart Resources, 1996.

Smith, James K. A. *You Are What You Love: The Spiritual Power of Habit.* Grand Rapids: Brazos Press, 2016.

Stark, Rodney. *The Rise of Christianity: A Sociologist Reconsiders History.* Princeton, NJ: Princeton University Press, 1996.

Walls, Andrew F. *The Missionary Movement in Christian History: Studies in the Transmission of Faith.* Maryknoll, NY: Orbis Books, 1996.

Willard, Dallas. *The Great Omission: Reclaiming Jesus's Essential Teachings on Discipleship.* San Francisco: HarperOne, 2006.

———. *The Spirit of the Disciplines: Understanding How God Changes Lives.* San Francisco: Harper & Row, 1988.

Yoder, John Howard. *The Politics of Jesus.* 2nd ed. Grand Rapids: Eerdmans, 1994.

Glossary of Terms

Accountability

A relational and spiritual practice in which leaders and believers invite trusted oversight, correction, and encouragement to ensure faithfulness, integrity, and growth in Christ.

Apostolic Oversight

Relational leadership modeled in the New Testament whereby seasoned leaders provide spiritual guidance, doctrinal clarity, and fatherly care to churches and pastors without coercive control.

Assignment

The specific calling, context, and responsibility God entrusts to a pastor or church. Assignment determines faithfulness; outcomes are God's responsibility.

Burden (Ministry Burden)

Pressure assumed by pastors when they carry expectations, metrics, or responsibilities God never assigned—often tied to numerical growth, comparison, or performance.

Calling

God's summons to serve Him in a particular role or context. Calling precedes visibility and remains valid regardless of outcomes or recognition.

Comparison

The act of measuring one's ministry against another's context, size, or outcomes. Scripture warns that comparison distorts wisdom and undermines obedience.

Contextual Growth

Growth that aligns with a church's geographic, cultural, relational, and seasonal realities. Healthy growth honors place, people, and timing rather than duplicating external models.

Discipleship

The lifelong process of forming believers into Christlikeness through teaching, obedience, relationship, and spiritual practice—not merely attendance or information transfer.

Discernment

Spiritual wisdom guided by Scripture and the Holy Spirit, enabling pastors to recognize God's will for their context, season, and assignment.

Endurance

Faithful perseverance in ministry over time, especially during slow, unseen, or discouraging seasons. Endurance is a spiritual discipline cultivated through trust and obedience.

Faithfulness

Consistent obedience to Christ in doctrine, character, and calling—regardless of visible results. Faithfulness is Scripture's primary measure of success.

Formation (Spiritual Formation)

The shaping of a believer's character, habits, and loves into the likeness of Christ. Formation emphasizes depth over speed and maturity over visibility.

Growth (Biblical Growth)

Increase—spiritual, relational, or numerical—that originates from God and follows faithfulness. Growth is fruit, not proof of worth or divine favor.

Hiddenness

The often-unseen nature of faithful ministry where obedience occurs without recognition. Scripture affirms that God sees and honors hidden faithfulness.

Leadership Capacity

The spiritual, emotional, relational, and organizational ability of leaders to steward responsibility well. Capacity must grow alongside influence to avoid burnout and harm.

Megaministry

A large-scale church or ministry, often measured by attendance or influence. Scripture does not present megaministry as a universal expectation for pastors.

Metrics

Tools used to measure aspects of ministry (attendance, giving, participation). When misused, metrics can replace biblical indicators such as love, obedience, and maturity.

Obedience

Faithful response to Christ's commands and calling. Obedience remains the core expectation of discipleship and leadership, regardless of outcome.

Pastor

A leader entrusted with preaching, teaching, prayer, and care for a congregation. The pastoral role emphasizes feeding the flock with God's Word.

Pastoral Burnout

Emotional, spiritual, and physical exhaustion often caused by misaligned expectations, overextension, isolation, or performance-driven ministry.

Pastoral Endurance

The grace-enabled ability to continue faithfully in ministry through seasons of discouragement, slow growth, or limited recognition.

Performance-Driven Ministry

A ministry posture focused on appearance, production, and approval rather than presence, formation, and obedience.

Quality vs. Quantity

A theological tension between depth of discipleship (quality) and numerical increase (quantity). Scripture prioritizes quality while trusting God with quantity.

Shepherd

A pastoral expression emphasizing presence, protection, guidance, and care for people. Shepherding focuses on relational depth rather than scale.

Small Church

A congregation with limited numerical size, often under 100

members. Scripture affirms that small churches can be faithful, healthy, and effective.

Spiritual Fatherhood

A mature leadership role characterized by generational vision, mentoring, and the raising of leaders rather than the accumulation of followers.

Stewardship

Faithful management of what God entrusts—people, resources, influence, and responsibility. Stewardship emphasizes trustworthiness over expansion.

Unseen Seasons

Periods of ministry where faithfulness is not accompanied by visible fruit or affirmation. Scripture teaches that unseen seasons often produce deep roots.

Visibility

Public recognition or platform. Visibility is not synonymous with effectiveness or faithfulness and must never replace obedience.

Well Done

The ultimate commendation from Christ, rooted in faithfulness rather than fame or results (Matthew 25:21).

Well Known

Public recognition or notoriety. Scripture does not equate being well known with being approved by God.

Yoke (Christ's Yoke)

Jesus' metaphor for shared responsibility under His lordship. His yoke is "easy" because it aligns believers with God's grace rather than self-imposed burden.

Study Questions by Chapter

Introduction – When Growth Becomes a Burden

1. How have you personally defined "success" in ministry over the years?
2. When did growth begin to feel like pressure rather than promise?
3. What expectations—spoken or unspoken—have shaped how you view your ministry?
4. How does Scripture challenge modern assumptions about church success?
5. What would it mean for you to fully release outcomes to God?

Chapter 1 – When Growth Becomes a Burden

1. In what ways have you felt responsible for results that may belong to God alone?
2. How has comparison—intentional or unintentional—affected your joy in ministry?
3. What burdens are you carrying now that Christ may not have placed on you?
4. How does Matthew 11:28–30 reframe your understanding of pastoral responsibility?
5. What would it look like to serve without constantly measuring outcomes?

Chapter 2 – Is Megaministry God's Will for Everyone?

1. Where did your expectations about church size originate—from Scripture or culture?

2. How does understanding "assignment" change the way you view your ministry context?
3. In what ways might pursuing someone else's vision create unnecessary strain?
4. How does Paul's ministry challenge a one-size-fits-all model of success?
5. What assignment has God clearly entrusted to you—not others?

Chapter 3 – What Jesus Actually Measures

1. What stands out to you about how Jesus evaluates the seven churches in Revelation?
2. Which of Christ's measurements—love, endurance, truth, repentance—most challenges you?
3. How does Jesus' evaluation differ from modern ministry metrics?
4. In what ways might reputation differ from spiritual reality in your context?
5. How would your leadership change if Christ's criteria were your primary guide?

Chapter 4 – Small Does Not Mean Stagnant

1. How have you subconsciously equated size with health or stagnation?
2. What strengths exist in your church because of its size?
3. How does Scripture affirm God's work in "small" or hidden places?
4. In what ways might smallness actually protect formation and discipleship?
5. How can you affirm the present season of your church without apology?

Chapter 5 — The Early Church Was Not a Franchise

1. How does the early church model challenge modern church growth assumptions?
2. What dangers arise when churches attempt to franchise ministry?
3. How does relational witness differ from attractional strategy?
4. In what ways has your church been shaped more by models than by mission?
5. What practices from the early church could strengthen your congregation today?

Chapter 6 — Quality, Quantity, and the Way of Jesus

1. How did Jesus handle crowds differently than modern leadership models encourage?
2. Where do you see tension between depth and speed in your ministry?
3. How might prioritizing quantity undermine long-term discipleship?
4. What practices help cultivate quality formation in your context?
5. How does obedience redefine what "fruitfulness" means for you?

Chapter 7 — Growth Tools Small Churches Often Overlook

1. What strengths already exist in your church that you may be undervaluing?
2. How does proximity enhance discipleship and pastoral care?
3. In what ways can leadership development happen relationally rather than programmatically?

4. How does prayer function practically in your church's growth and health?
5. Which overlooked tool do you sense God inviting you to steward more intentionally?

Chapter 8 – When Growth Goes Wrong

1. Have you experienced growth that arrived before readiness? What happened?
2. What warning signs indicate that growth may be outpacing formation?
3. How can leadership development be paced wisely alongside growth?
4. What safeguards protect the soul of the pastor during seasons of expansion?
5. How can growth be stewarded as responsibility rather than reward?

Chapter 9 – Church Shenanigans to Avoid

1. Which "shenanigans" described in this chapter felt most familiar or convicting?
2. How have trends influenced your ministry decisions—positively or negatively?
3. Where might performance have subtly replaced presence in your leadership?
4. What practices need reevaluation through a biblical lens?
5. How can simplicity restore health and joy to ministry?

Chapter 10 – Healthy Growth Is Contextual

1. How does your local context shape what faithfulness looks like?
2. What assumptions have you imported from other ministry environments?

3. How does honoring seasonality change expectations for growth?
4. What metrics best reflect health in your specific setting?
5. How can discernment replace duplication moving forward?

Chapter 11 — From Pastor to Shepherd to Father

1. Which leadership role—pastor, shepherd, or father—best describes your current season?
2. What dangers arise from skipping stages of leadership maturity?
3. How does spiritual fatherhood differ from positional authority?
4. In what ways are you intentionally raising other leaders?
5. How does leadership maturity affect the burden you carry?

Chapter 12 — When Faithfulness Leads to Increase

1. How do you distinguish between trusting God for increase and striving for it?
2. What biblical examples reshape your understanding of timing and fruitfulness?
3. How can increase be received without reintroducing pressure?
4. What structures and disciplines protect the soul during growth?
5. How do you redefine success after seasons of expansion?

Chapter 13 — A Word to the Discouraged Pastor

1. What forms of discouragement have you carried silently?
2. How does Scripture normalize weariness without condemning it?
3. In what ways has comparison intensified discouragement for you?

4. What does obedience without applause look like in your daily ministry?
5. What would it mean to keep going with renewed trust?

Conclusion – Well Done Is Greater Than Well Known

1. How has this book reshaped your understanding of success?
2. What false measures are you ready to release permanently?
3. How does Christ's "well done" reframe your motivation for ministry?
4. What practices will help you finish faithfully rather than famously?
5. What legacy of obedience do you hope to leave behind?

ABOUT THE AUTHOR

Bishop Antonio M. Palmer is the Senior Pastor of Kingdom Celebration Center and the Presiding Bishop of Kingdom Alliance of Churches International, overseeing a global network of 81 churches. With a ministry rooted in the Gospel since 1993, he planted his first church in Annapolis, Maryland, in 1995 and became a beacon of leadership, service, and transformation.

A passionate advocate for missions, Bishop Palmer leads leadership conferences, plants churches, and provides humanitarian aid to thousands of children in need across the globe. His work includes substantial financial support for orphanages in India and East Africa, demonstrating a steadfast commitment to serving the underserved.

Bishop Palmer, a respected community leader, is celebrated for fostering unity and collaboration among diverse groups. His efforts address critical issues, promote meaningful dialogue, and inspire transformative change. He holds a Bachelor of Divinity, Master's in Pastoral Counseling, and a Doctorate of Divinity. He has been recognized with numerous accolades, including two Governor Citations, two County Executive Citations, Dr. Martin Luther King Jr. Drum Major Award, and the Presidential Lifetime Achievement Award.

As an entrepreneur, Bishop Palmer owns Kingdom Publishing LLC, Antonio Marlin Art, and Kingdom Kare, Inc., a thriving nonprofit organization. He is also the author of ten more impactful books:

- The Irrevocable Covenant
- When We Were Them
- Sacred or Syncretized?
- Divine Manifestations: Angels and Theophanies in Biblical Studies
- Rooted and Grounded in Love [Anthology]
- Living By the Spirit
- Love Thyself: Empowering Men for Healthy Living
- God's Rest Revealed: A Life Flowing with Milk and Honey
- Building an Effective Prayer Life
- Mark the Perfect Man: How to Find a Model of Maturity
- Revival: God Will Come Where You Are
- Little Kairo Takes on the World (Children's Book)

To contact the author, please email him at:
Godwillcome2U@gmail.com